The STUDENT'S INSTRUCTOR In Drawing And Working THE FIVE ORDERS Of ARCHITECTURE

Peter Nicholson

1815

The Toolemera Press
History Preserved

www.toolemera.com

The Student's Instructor In Drawing And Working The Five Orders Of Architecture
The Fourth Edition
by Peter Nicholson
J. Taylor: At The Architectural Library, No. 59, High Holborn
(London, Great Britain)
1815

No part of this book may be reproduced, stored in an electronic retrieval system, or transmitted in any form or by an means, electronic, mechanical, photocopy, photographic or otherwise without the written permission of the publisher.

Excerpts of one page or less for the purposes of review and comment are permissible.

Copyright © 2013 The Toolemera Press
All rights reserved.

International Standard Book Number
ISBN : 978-0-9897477-2-1
Trade Paper

Published by
The Toolemera Press
Massachusetts, U.S.A.

www.toolemera.com

Manufactured in the United States of America

Introduction

Peter Nicholson, 1765-1844

Peter Nicholson was born and raised in Scotland and lived in England. At an early age, his primarily self-taught proficiency in mathematics, as well as his innate artistic skills as displayed in his drawings of local mills and factories, indicated the direction for his future professional life.

Initially entering into training with his father, a stone mason, a trade he found not to his liking, Nicholson subsequently left for an apprenticeship as a cabinet-maker, completing the apprenticeship as well as working as a journeyman in Edinburgh, Scotland, and London, England. While pursuing his journeyman tasks, Nicholson secured a position as a teacher of mathematics and geometry at a school for mechanical engineers. Nicholson excelled to such an extent at this work that he left cabinet-work to begin a new career as an educator and author of architectural and technical books.

At the age of 27, in 1792, Nicholson authored and engraved the plates for *The Carpenter's New Guide*. He went on to write *The Student's Instructor In Drawing And Working The Five Orders Of Architecture* in 1795, *The Carpenter and Joiner's Assistant* in 1797, and 24 more titles on architecture and related subjects. During Nicholson's lifetime, his books were essential to the libraries of beginning as well as experienced builders and architects.

Nicholson established his own school in London for the instruction of mathematics, architecture, surveying and modern building technologies, particularly those that he had invented or espoused. While Nicholson was contracted to supervise various building projects, it was through his work as an architectural historian and theorist that his fame was established.

The Student's Instructor In The Five Orders Of Architecture

The Student's Instructor was a standard reference book for the student of architecture and architectural drawing as well as for the practical carpenter of the late 18th century through the middle of the 19th century. The five orders of architecture refer to the book of the same title published in 1562 by Giacomo Barozzi da Vignolo in which he described the classic architectural elements of Doric, Ionic, Corinthian (Grecian), Tuscan and Composite (Roman).

These five orders, or design elements, have for centuries served as the foundations of the architectural designs of American, British and European buildings.

More Toolemera Reprints

- Mechanick Exercises: Joseph Moxon 1703
- The Mechanic's Companion: Peter Nicholson 1850
- The Circle Of The Mechanical Arts: Thomas Martin 1813
- The Complete Cabinet-Maker's And Upholsterer's Guide: J. Stokes 1829
- The Book Of Swedish Home Sloyd: Anna Petersson Berg 1925
- The Teacher's Hand-Book Of Slojd: Otto Salomon 1891
- A Manual Of Wood Carving: Charles G. Leland, Revised by John J. Holtzapffel 1891
- Wood Carving: Joseph Phillips 1896
- Wood Turning On The Foot Treadle Lathe: William Fairham 1922
- Woodwork Tools And How To Use Them: William Fairham 1922
- Woodwork Joints: William Fairham 1920
- Cabinet Construction: J. C. S. Brough 1930
- Furniture Making: Advanced Projects In Woodwork: Ira Griffith 1912
- The Painter, Gilder, And Varnisher's Companion: H. C. Baird 1850
- Our Workshop: Temple Thorold 1866
- Carpentry And Joinery For Amateurs: James Lukin 1879
- The Art Of Mitring: Owen Maginnis 1892
- Working Drawings Of Colonial Furniture: F. Bryant 1922

www.shop.toolemera.com

Toolemera Press

The Toolemera Press reprints classic books on early crafts, trades and industries carefully selected from the shelves of our personal library. We contract with the Ingram Group - Lightning Source Print-On-Demand service to keep retail prices affordable.

www.shop.toolemera.com

THE
STUDENT'S INSTRUCTOR
IN DRAWING AND WORKING
THE FIVE ORDERS
OF
ARCHITECTURE.

FULLY EXPLAINING THE BEST METHODS
FOR STRIKING REGULAR AND QUIRKED MOULDINGS;

FOR DIMINISHING AND GLUEING OF
COLUMNS AND CAPITALS;

FOR FINDING THE TRUE DIAMETER OF AN
ORDER TO ANY GIVEN HEIGHT;

FOR STRIKING THE IONIC VOLUTE,
CIRCULAR OR ELLIPTICAL;

WITH FINISHED

Examples, on a large Scale,

OF

THE ORDERS, THEIR PLANCEERS, &c.

AND SOME

DESIGNS FOR DOOR-CASES,

ELEGANTLY ENGRAVED ON FORTY-ONE PLATES.

WITH EXPLANATIONS.

By PETER NICHOLSON, ARCHITECT.

AUTHOR OF THE CARPENTER'S NEW GUIDE, CARPENTER AND JOINER'S
ASSISTANT, &c.

THE FOURTH EDITION
CONSIDERABLY AUGMENTED AND IMPROVED.

LONDON:
PUBLISHED BY J. TAYLOR,
AT THE ARCHITECTURAL LIBRARY,
NO. 59, HIGH HOLBORN.

1815.

Printed by W. Stratford, Crown Court, Temple Bar.

PREFACE

TO THE THIRD EDITION.

THE usefulness of this little volume has been fully proved by the great numbers which have been sold: a new Edition being now called for, I have examined the work throughout, and have made such corrections and additions, as appeared to be necessary to adapt it to the prevailing style of architecture: to this purpose I have given a new plate containing a variety of *Modern Mouldings*, also six new ones of *Antique Doric Capitals* and entablatures, with the parts at large and in detail: so that in this small work every member of these specimens of ancient magnificence is equally clear, and distinct, as in the large work of the original author, and as I have reduced the proportions to the modular scale, are more easily put in practice. Upon the whole, it will be found that the Greek Doric which has of late been so much in vogue, is

fully

fully explained and elucidated: I have also given an example of a chaste and noble Ionic Capital, all these are selected from Stuart's elegant and interesting work on the Antiquities of Athens; the other new plates are an outline of the Composite Capital for the use of learners, and an antique Ionic Door case, proper to be drawn from or worked. These additions, on ten new plates with various corrections in the descriptions, render this edition more complete and useful; and I think there is now nothing wanting to constitute it a complete introduction to the orders of architecture both ancient and modern.

1810.

PREFACE.

THE following Treatise will be found particularly useful to Students in Architecture: It contains a complete developement of the methods of drawing and working the five orders, which may be said to be the foundation, the very ABC of the art of building: as from these, with their several proportions and variations, arises all that is great, elegant, or harmonious in the noblest structure, wherefore I most earnestly recommend to the student, to obtain a thorough knowledge of every order, its parts, proportions, and entire figure, as being absolutely necessary to ALL who aspire to eminence in this profession:

To this purpose the following work is well adapted, and gives in the most detailed and accurate manner, examples of the five orders, their proportions and enrichments, according to the present taste; which are so completely explained by the lines, and the measurement on the plates, that a little attention will enable every person readily to comprehend the proportion, use, and situation of each member: and also the several methods adopted in calculating the parts, and for setting them off on rods for practice, to any scale. The manner of drawing them on paper is fully explained, and I must here advise the student to make a diligent practice of drawing the outlines to a large scale, so that the measures may apply

with

with accuracy, before he proceeds to finish in shading, by so doing, he will acquire a facility of manner, and an accuracy of eye in judging of the beauties of proportion, which will ever be of essential use to him.

The explanation of the Tuscan order is given very full, and as the same methods apply to each of the other orders, they are not repeated. It is scarcely necessary to observe, the height of the several columns is given according to the most esteemed masters; nevertheless they may with much propriety be varied, to suit particular purposes, or situations.

The method of describing quirked mouldings is new and easy for practice, for any swell. I have shewn a new method for striking the Ionic volute, which will produce that spiral curve with more elegance and regularity in the sweep, than by any other method I have seen.

That important branch of practice, glueing up of columns and capitals, is shewn in a new and accurate manner, easy to be understood. I have also shewn new and easy methods for diminishing of columns, and for marking the flutes and fillets on them and on pilasters; which, with various other interesting matters, will, I hope, make the operative parts of the five orders in theory and in practice, be better understood than by any former publication.

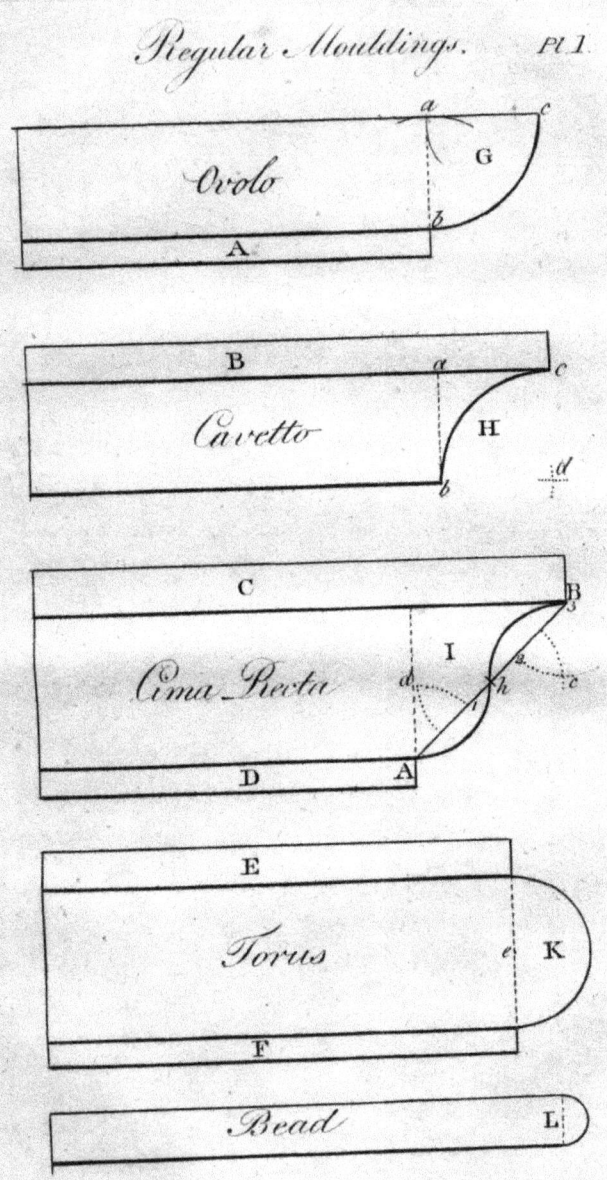

EXPLANATIONS, &c.

PLATE I.
TO DESCRIBE THE SEVERAL KINDS OF MOULDINGS.

To describe an Ovolo, take the height *a b*; set the compasses in *b*, describe an arc, and with the same distance on the projection at *c*, describe an arc cutting the former at *a*, then on *a*, as a center; describe an arc *b c*, and the ovolo will be completed.

To describe a Cavetto, on *b*, with the height *a b*; describe an arc on the projection at *c*, with the same distance describe another arc cutting the former at *d*; then with the same extension on *d*, describe the arc *b c*, and it will be a cavetto.

To describe a Cima Recta, join the projections at each end by the right line A B, divide it into two equal parts at *h*, and in order to make it look bold, divide A B into three equal parts, or nearly so, and with one third, on A and *h* as centres, describe arcs, cutting each other at *d*; and in the same manner find the intersection, on the opposite side of the line at *c*; lastly on *d*, and *c*, describe the arcs A *h*, and *h* B, and it will form the cima recta required.

To describe the Torus, divide the height into two equal parts at *e*, and on *e*, as a center, describe a semicircle to that height; and it will form a torus.

The *Bead* is formed as the Torus.

Note, These are the forms of regular mouldings, viz. the height equal to the projection: but there are other forms, where the projection is often less than the height, and the curvature of the moulding much flatter; however the same methods for describing the one, will do for the other.

PLATE II.

MODERN OR QUIRKED MOULDINGS.

To describe the Cima Reversa A, join the projections at *a,* and *b,* by the line *a b,* and proceed in the same manner as with the cima recta before described.

To describe a quirked Cima Reversa B, divide the perpendicular height into seven parts; with two of the parts describe a semicircle *c e ;* on *a* draw a line from *e c,* and on the height of the first division from the bottom *b,* describe the arc *c d,* and it will compleat the moulding.

The quirked Cima Reversa C, is described in a similar manner; as is plain on inspection.

To describe a quirked Ovolo D, divide the height into four equal parts, with one part on *c,* describe the arc *a f g.* Join *c b* to the end of the fillet below; on *b* describe the arc *c d,* on *c,* with the distance *a b,* describe an arc cutting the former at *d;* through *d,* and *c,* draw the line *d c f,* cutting the small circle at *f;* then with a radius, *d f,* describe the arc *f b,* and it will compleat a quirked ovolo.

To describe the quirked Moulding E, flatter in the lower part than that at D, describe the smaller circle as in the last; and through its center, and the end *b* of the fillet, draw the line *c b e,* taking the point *e,* according as you intend to have the under part of the moulding, flatter or quicker: take the distance *e c,*

and

Modern Mouldings. Pl. 2

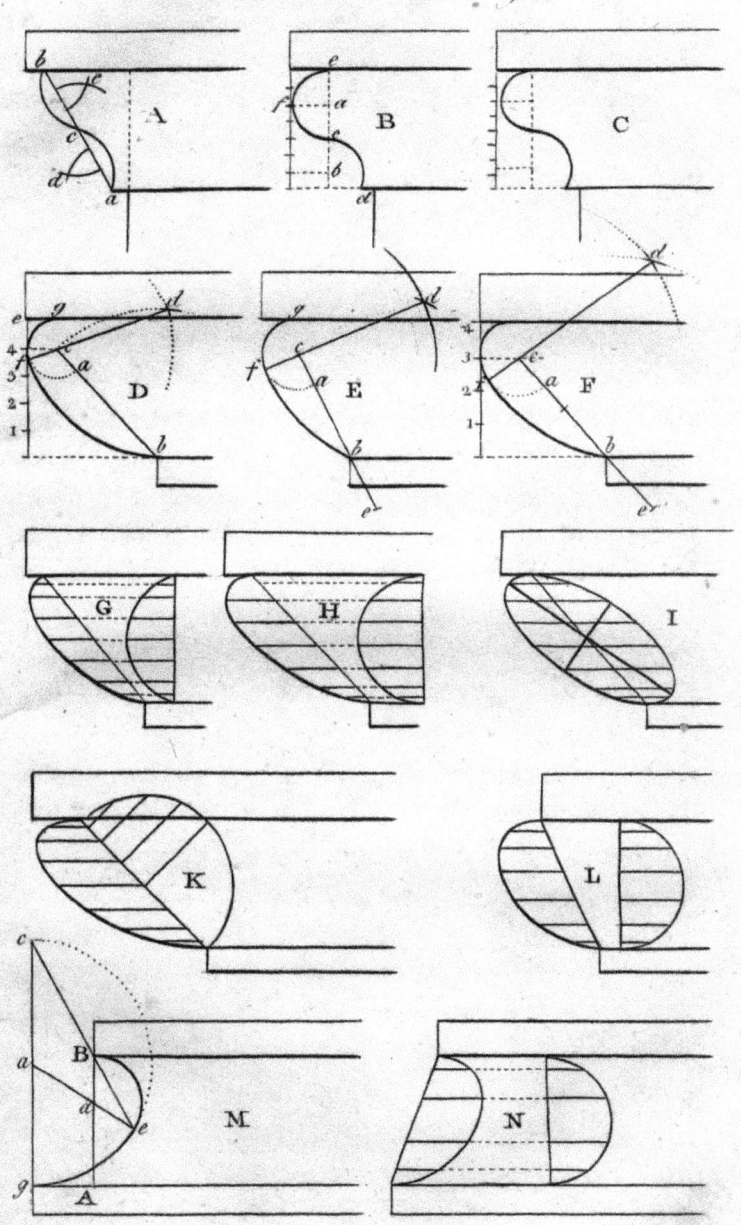

and on *b*, describe an arc at *d*, then take the distance *e a*, that is *e c*, made less by the radius *c a*, of the smaller arc *a f g*, on *c*, with that distance, describe an arc cutting the former at *d*; lastly on *d*, with a radius *d f*, describe the arc *f b*, and it will complete the quirked ovolo required.

> *Note*, The quirked ovolo at F, is described in the same manner as E; the only difference being in the projection, which is greater.

These are the most proper for the workman's purpose, though various other methods may be shewn to answer the same purpose; as G, H, I, K, which are traced from a semicircle, by applying the same projections to a line of any inclination required.

G, is a torus moulding taken from a semicircle; and may be applied where the projection of the upper fillet is greater than the projection of the lower.

To describe a Scotia M, from the top of the fillet draw B A, perpendicular, cutting the bottom of the fillet at A: from *g* the end of the bottom fillet; draw the line *g a c*, parallel to A B: make *g a*, equal to twice *g* A, on *a*: describe the semicircle *g e c*, cutting the line *g a c*, at *c*, through *c*, and the end of the fillet, at B, draw the line *c* B *e*, cutting the semicircle at *e*: draw the line *a d e*, cutting A B, in *d*; lastly on *d*, describe the arc, *e* B, and it will complete the scotia.

N is a scotia, described by a similar method to the ovolos G, H, I, K, *viz*. through points found from a semicircle, to the height of the moulding.

PLATE III.

MODERN MOULDINGS.

To describe a Grecian Ovolo or Echinus, have two tangents to the curve, and the points of contact given, one of the points of contact being the greatest projection, and the other the lower extremity of the curve.

Fig. 1, 2, 3, let A B, B C, be the two tangents, A, the point of contact at the greatest projection, and C, the lower extremity of the curve; draw A E, parallel to B C, and C E, parallel to B A; produce C E, to F, making E F, equal to E C; divide A E, and A B, each into the same number of equal parts; from the point F, draw lines through the points of division in A E, and also from the point C, draw lines to the points of division in A B, to meet the others through the divisions of A E; through the intersections draw a curve, which will be the contour of the ovolo required.

OBSERVATIONS.

The moulding will be flatter or quicker according as the point B, the extremity of the tangent B C, is nearer or more remote from A, the greatest projection. In *Fig.* 1, B D, is one half of A D; in *Fig.* 2, B D, is one third of A D; and in *Fig.* 3, B D, is one fourth of A D. Also the quirk or recess at the top will be greater, as the distance A G is greater, A G, being in the same straight line with A D.

The same things being given, to describe the moulding to any of the conic sections.

Fig. 4. Draw A H, parallel to the fillets; produce the vertical line C H, to K, making H K, equal H C, and

Modern Mouldings.

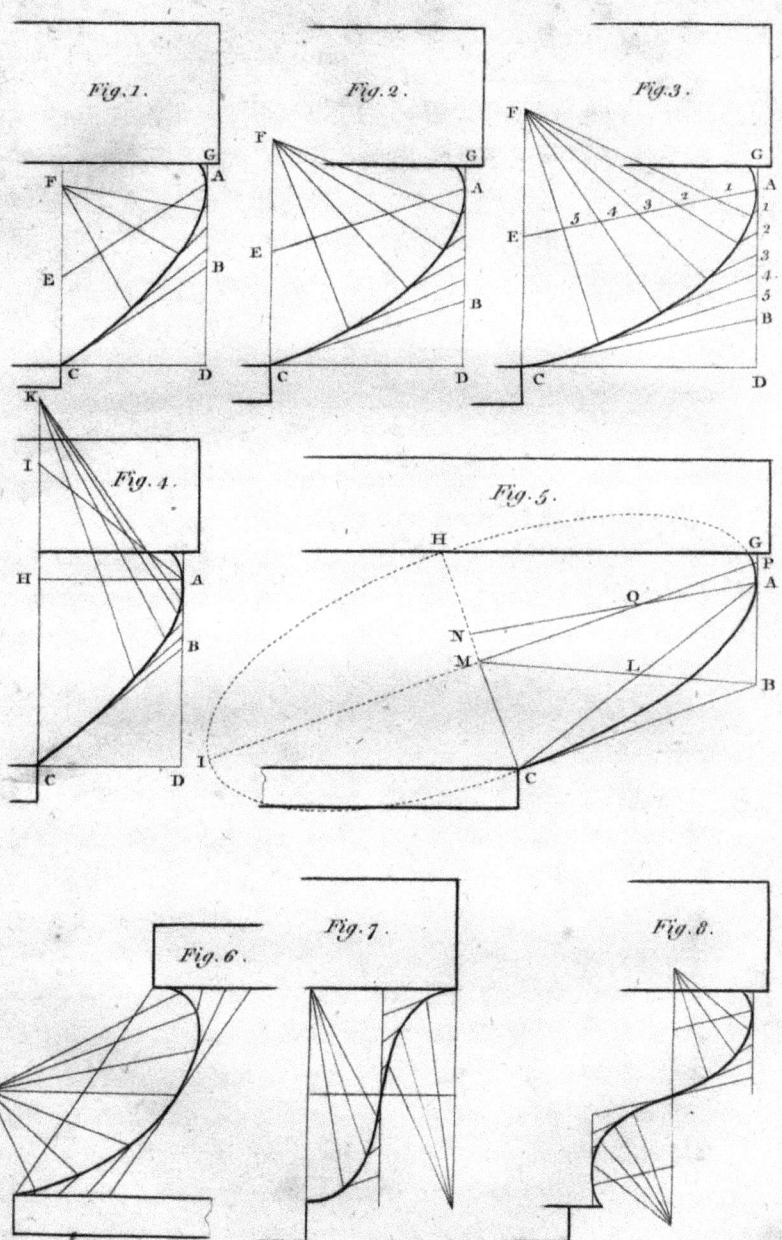

and H I, equal to B D: join A I; divide A I, and A B, each into the same number of equal parts, and through the points of division in these lines, and through the points K, and C, draw lines to meet each other, and through these points draw a curve, and it will be the ovolo required.

OBSERVATION.

If B D, were less than the half of A D, the moulding would be elliptical; and if BD, were equal to the half of A D, the moulding would be parabolical. In this example B D, is greater than the half of A D, the moulding is hyperbolical. Of this form is the echinus in all the Grecian doric capitals, except the Doric Portico at Athens, in which the echinus of the capital is elliptical.

The same things being given to describe the echinus, the point C being the extremity of one of the axis.

Fig. 5. join A C, and bisect it in L; draw B, L, M, C M, perpendicular to B C, and P M, parallel to B C: with the distance C M, on the point A, describe an arc cutting P M, at O: produce C M, to N, and draw A, O, N; make N P, equal to A N, and M P, and M will be the two semi-axis by which the curve may be described.

Fig. 6. *is a Scotia or Trochillus,* the fillets may be considered as tangents, and the line parallel to the line joining the fillet as another tangent. *Fig.* 7. a cima-recta, compounded of two quarters of an ellipse upon the axes. *Fig.* 8. a cima-reversa, compounded of two quarters of an ellipse from conjugate diameters, which are given in position. These are described upon similar principles to figures 1, 2, and 3.

PLATE IV.

TO MAKE A RULE FOR DIMINISHING THE SHAFT OF A COLUMN.

Method 1st. *Fig.* 1. describe a semicircle, on the bottom of the column A B, from the top of the column, draw the line E 4, parallel to the axis D C, or middle line of the column, cutting the semicircle at the base in 4; divide the arc A 4, into four, or any other number of equal parts, and divide the height C D, into the same number of equal parts; as 1, 2, 3, through the divisions 1, 2, 3, 4, of the semicircle at the base, draw lines 1 *a*, 2 *b*, 3 *c*, and 4 *d*, parallel to A B; set off those parts from each side of the axis, on the corresponding numbers on the shaft; then by bending a thin lath or slip, round pins or nails fixt in these points, you will have the contour, or curve of the column: and the reverse of this will be the edge of the rule for working it by.

Method, 2d. *Fig.* 2. divide the height of the diminishing rule, as A B, into any number of equal parts; as four, at 1, 2, 3, and divide the difference of the semidiameter C D, at the top and bottom, into the same number, *viz.* four, and draw lines from each division on C D, towards E, at the bottom; cutting lines drawn parallel to the base, through 1, 2, 3, will give points, by which you may draw as before, a curve of a very regular and pleasing form, which may be drawn on the edge of the rule, or on the column itself, as is most convenient for the workman; this, in my opinion, is much preferable to the first method.

Fig. 3. shews the same thing not in its just proportion but clearer to inspection, as the divisions are much larger.

PLATE

TO DRAW THE FLUTES OF COLUMNS

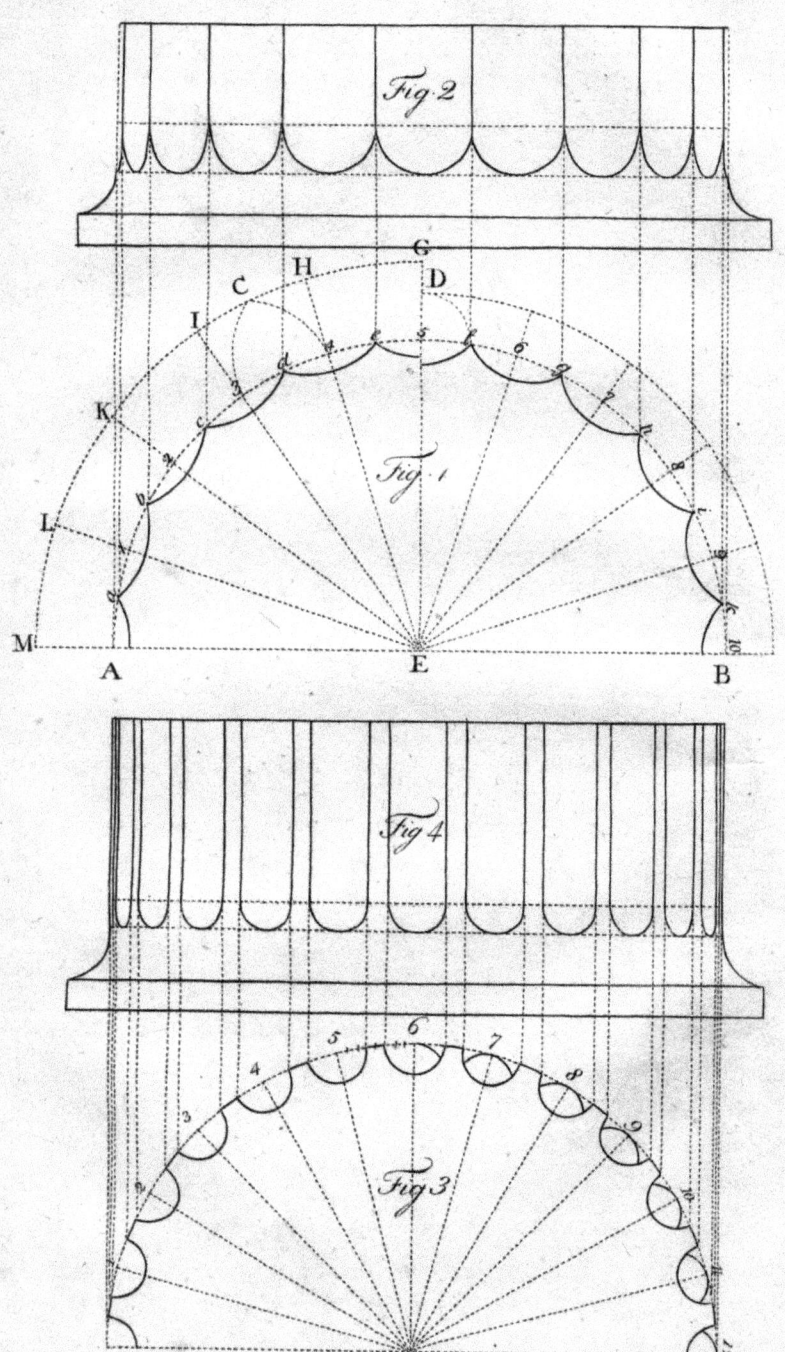

PLATE V.

TO DRAW THE FLUTES OF COLUMNS.

To draw the flutes of the Doric Column. On A B, *Fig.* 1. the diameter of the column, describe a semicircle, and divide the semicircle into ten equal parts; (as the doric column usually contains twenty flutes, which are in general made shallow, and without fillets;) through every two of the divisions draw lines E 1, E 2, E 3, E 4, to E 10, between any two divisions (as 3 and 4) describe two arcs whose vertex is C: on E with a radius E C, describe the quadrant G, H, I, K, L, M, cutting the lines E A, E 1, E 2, E 3, E 4, &c. in the points, G, H, I, K, L, M, which are the centers for the flutes; but if the flutes are wanted deeper, you may make the distance 5 D, half the breadth of a flute; and proceed as shewn on the other quadrant, and from *a, b, c,* &c. draw perpendiculars to the bottom of the column.

Fig. 2. *The Ionic, Corinthian, and Composite orders,* have in general twenty-four flutes, with a fillet between each; (the fillet one third of a flute,) in order to have that number, and preserve the just proportion of a flute to a fillet, observe the following rule, divide the semicircumference, *Fig.* 3. into twelve equal parts, at 1, 2, 3, 4, 5, &c. to 12, divide any division into eight equal parts, as that between 5 and 6, then take three of these parts, and on 1, 2, 3, &c. to 12, as centers; describe arcs which are nearly semicircular as in the plate, and then draw them to the column, *Fig.* 4.

PLATE VI.

TO DRAW THE FLUTES AND FILLETS ROUND THE SHAFT OF A COLUMN.

If the columns are of stone, or wood, the whole or any part may be fluted in the following manner; after being properly rounded, and the end or joints made parallel to each other, find the centers of the circles at each end; and if they are not already found, cut two holes, directly in the middle at each end perpendicular to the joints, so that the centers shall be in the middle of the holes; this being done, drive in two pieces of wood, so as to be quite tight in the holes, and to project out about five or six inches; let the projecting parts be well rounded off, so as to be exactly in the middle of the ends; then make a diminishing rule as in plate 4. To fit the curve of the column, let the ends of this diminishing rule be fixed into two pieces, $a\ b$; which are made to revolve round the pins at the ends by means of notches, or any other convenient way; so that the curved edge of the rule be very near to the curved surface of the column; and one side of the rule to tend exactly to the center: to keep the rule steady from bending sideways, fix a rule to the other side, the whole length of the diminishing rule, of a sufficient strength to keep the diminishing rule from bending; so that the breadths of the two rules will be at right angles to each other, the two end pieces and diminishing rule being fixed fast together; the whole may be turned round the pins at the ends as centers, like one entire piece: then the operation of drawing the flutes and fillets will be as follows: suppose it were required to flute the Ionic, Corinthian

To draw the flutes & fillets on the Shaft of a Column.

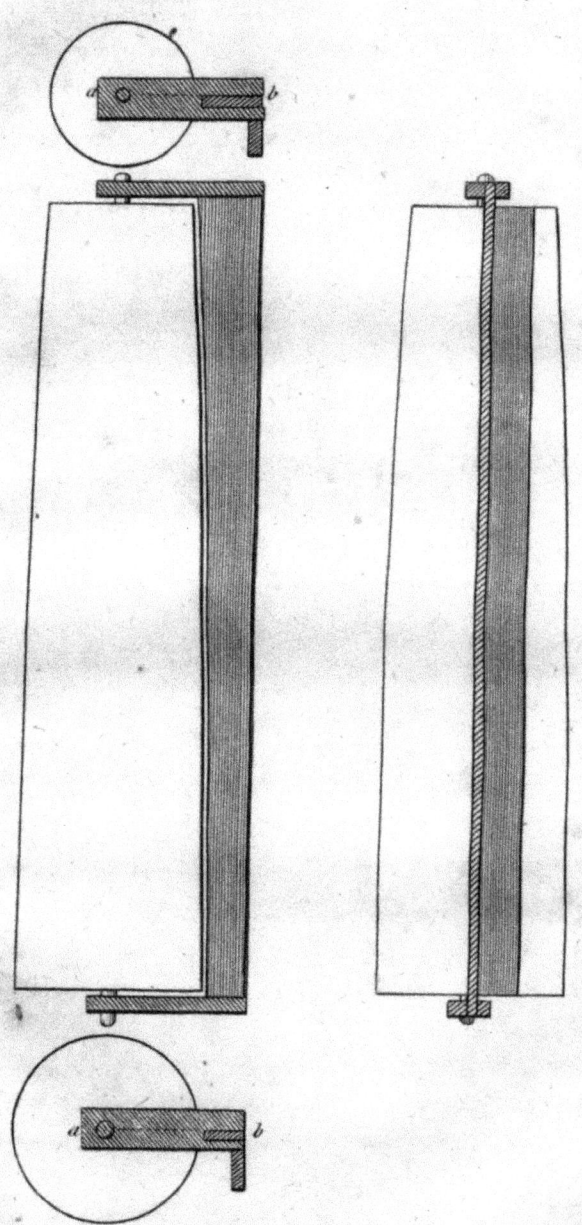

rinthian, or **Composite** columns, the circumference at either end will be divided into six equal parts, by taking half the diameter at that end, and applying it round the said circumference; then each of these divisions being divided into four, the whole circumference will be divided into twenty-four: in order to have the proportion of a flute to a fillet as 1, to 3, divide any one of the last divisions into four equal parts, and one of these parts will be the breadth of a fillet, which being set off from the same side of each division, the whole column will be divided into flutes, and fillets, then by turning the rule round to each mark, or division, you may make a piece of sharp steel draw on the shaft of the column the flutes, and fillets, to the greatest exactness, by keeping it close to the side of the rule.

This method is by far the most ready, as well as the most correct of any that I have yet seen; this machine is shewn complete on the plate, and I hope a careful inspection will render it sufficiently plain; there are other methods of drawing the flutes on the shaft of a column, as by drawing two parallel lines through the center at each end of the column, and dividing the circumferences at the ends into the number of flutes and fillets, then bending a thin rule from the respective divisions at each end; it is necessary to be careful that, the edge of the rule by which you draw, touch the curved surface of the column only: but this method, however simple, is very liable to error. The methods that some workmen make use of for setting off the flutes and fillets round the shaft of a column, are as follow:

C PLATE

PLATE VII.

TO DRAW THE FLUTES AND FILLETS ON A COLUMN OR PILASTER.

Fig. 1. A B, is any line divided into flutes, and fillets, greater than the circumference of the column at the base; on A B, describe the equilateral triangle A B G, draw all the points in A B, to G, then if G C, and G D, are equal to the circumference of the column at the bottom of the shaft, the line C D, will be equal to the same circumference; lay a piece of parchment, or any thing that is pliable, on C D, and mark all the flutes and fillets on it, then apply this round the column at the bottom, and prick them round it, divide the circumference at top in the same manner as E F, and draw the flutes with a thin rule as before.

Fig. 2. is another method for marking the flutes and fillets round the ends of the column; the line A B, is a line divided into flutes and fillets, less than the circumference of the top part of the column; draw any number of parallel lines from the divisions of A B, let B C, B D, B E, be the top or bottom diameter; set one foot of the compasses in B, and cross the line A F, at C, D, or E, draw the line B C, B D, or B E, and either will be divided into flutes, and fillets, as before.

Let A B, be the breadth of the pilaster, draw any line A C; take your compasses at any convenient opening, and run twenty-nine times the said opening from A, to C, and join B C, then set your bevel to the angle A C B, and from the points on A C, draw lines cutting A B, as is shewn by the figure, and from the points on A B, draw the flutes and fillets with a common gauge.

There

To draw the flutes on a Column or Pilaster. Pl. 7.

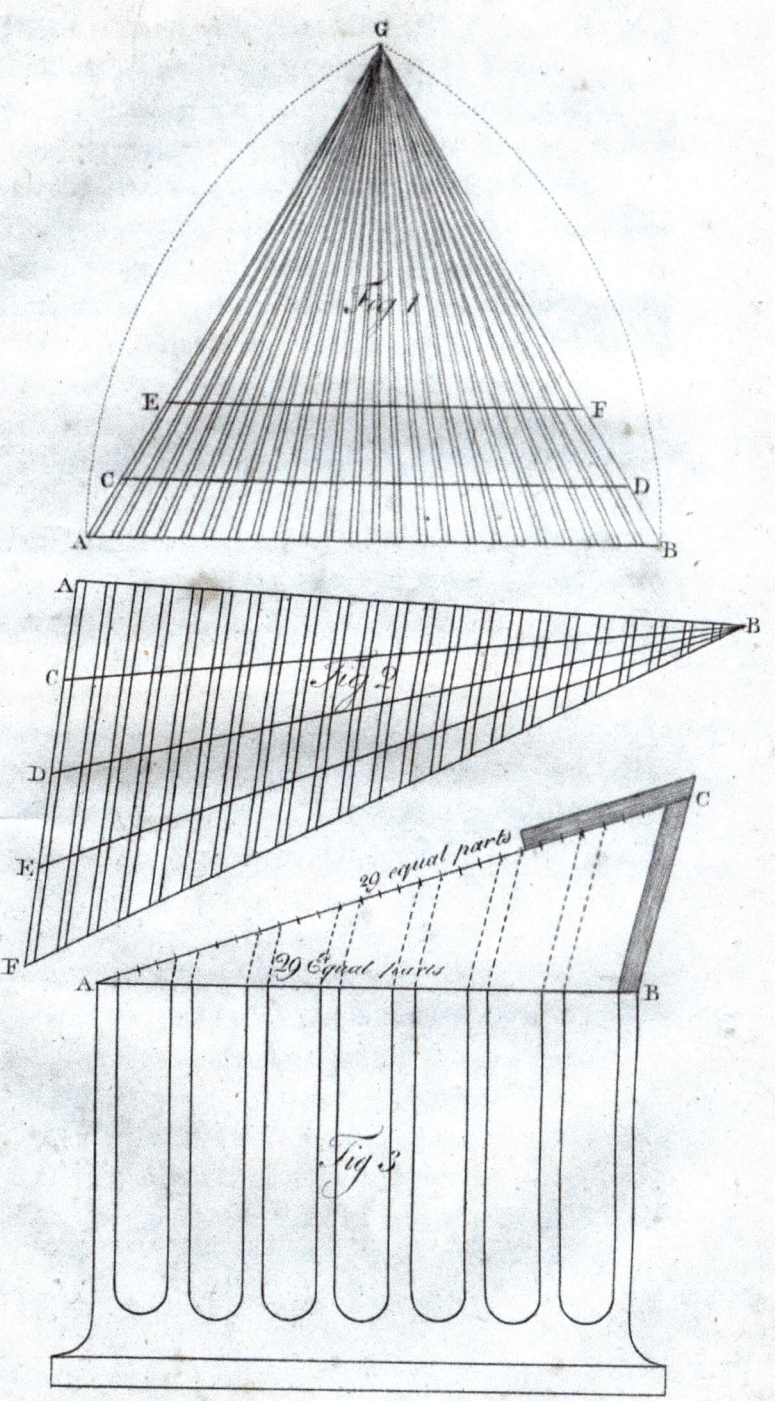

There is another method of drawing the flutes of a diminished pilaster with one gauge, and at one movement, by making the gauge equal to the width of the bottom, or something wider; but as this method is erroneous in its principle no diagram is exhibited.

The best method to draw the flutes on a diminished pilaster: is to divide the height of the trunk into any convenient number of equal parts on a longitudinal line passing through the middle of the breadth at top and bottom, and through the points of division draw transverse lines to the longitudinal line; set off the flutes and fillets on each transverse line: take nails or brads in each corresponding point of each transverse line and bend a pliable slip of wood round the nails, and draw a line and proceed till every set of corresponding points are used, and the pilaster will have its face drawn for flutes as required.

PLATE VIII.

TO GLUE UP THE SHAFT OF A COLUMN.

This must be glued up in eight or more staves, according to the bigness of the column, but always observe to have the joint in the middle of a fillet, and not in a flute, as it would very much weaken it; in this plate is shewn the plan of the top and bottom ends, or the horizontal section at each end. If eight pieces are sufficient for the column, you must describe an octagon round the ends, then draw lines from each angle of the octagon to the center, and it will give the bevil of the edges of the staves for the joints, which must be quite straight from top to bottom; only, that the staves be narrower at the top, as is shewn by the plans of the column; the staves must be of a sufficient thickness, because the outside is to be curved to the swell of the column; by means of a diminishing rule: then proceed to glue the pieces together one after the other as the glue dries; block them well at the corners in the inside, which will greatly strengthen the joints: proceed in this manner to the last stave; the blocks must be glued on and dried before you can glue your last stave in: or you may glue pieces quite across for the last stave, fixed to the inside of the two adjoining staves, or by screws fix them to each stave, then the underside of your last stave must be planned so as to rub well on the cross pieces, and when the stave is put in, and glued upon the said cross pieces, you may drive it tight home like a wedge, and the whole will be as firm as possible; but care must be taken that the staves and blocks are quite dry, otherwise the column after some time will be in danger of coming to pieces at the joints: in glueing each piece, care must be taken to try it to the plan, or backing mould, as a trifling difference in each will make a very sensible error in going round the column after the glueing; when the glue in the columns is dry, you may proceed to work off the angles regularly all round, the column will then have double the number of sides, or cants; proceed in the same manner working off the angles as before, so as to make the column have its sides, or cants, quite regular; lastly, make a plane to fit the curve of the column at the bottom, or rather flatter; then round off all the angles, until the surface of the column is quite smooth: there is, however, one thing I would observe in respect to the moulds for jointing the staves together; that is, they are

not

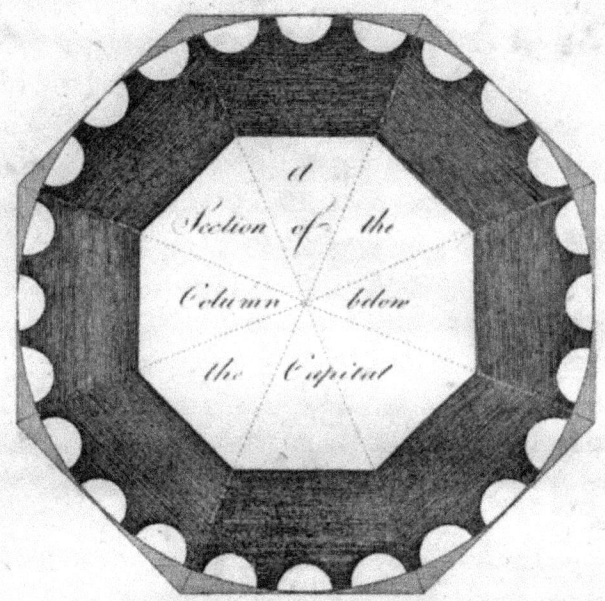

The manner of Gluing up the shafts of a Column

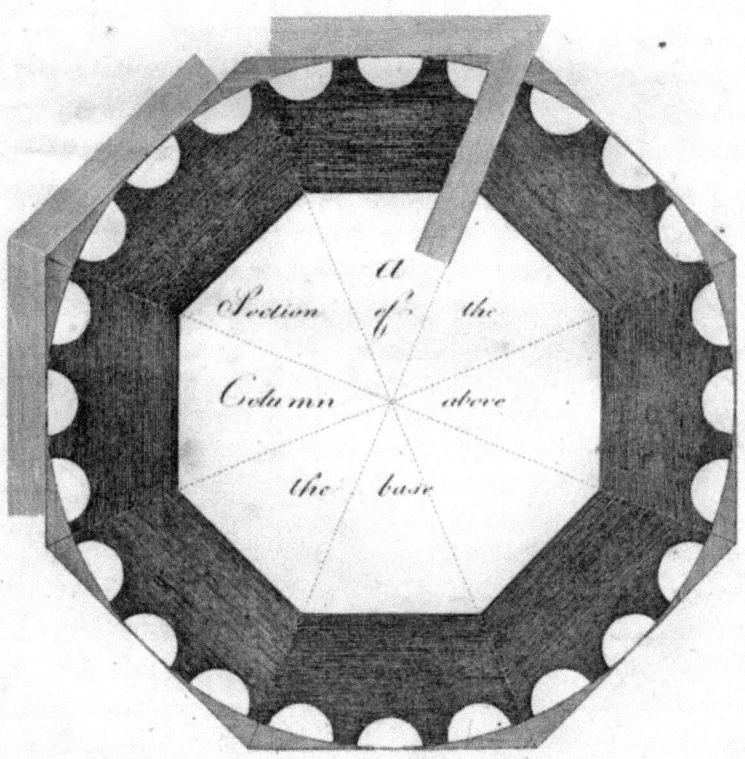

not exactly true when applied in a direction perpendicular to the joint; the proper method to find them true is in the same manner as you will find the backing of a hip rafter, or of a pitch skylight; but, however, this exactness is not always attended to, as the deviation from the truth is so small as to be disregarded: after your column is quite finished it ought to be well painted, so as to preserve it from being injured by the weather.

Another method is, glue the column in two halves, and then glue these together; the blockings may be put in a considerable way by hand; but if the column is too long, a rod of sufficient length may be used. Either of these methods have inconveniences which cannot be avoided, by the former method the last joints cannot be rubbed together because of the tapering of the stave, but if it is glued quickly, it will be pretty sound: by the latter method there will an uncertainty of the blockings being sound.

Note, The grain of the blocking pieces must be the same way as the grain of the column, that if affected by weather, they may expand alike.

For the method of glueing up Bases, see Plate XXXVIII. and description.

PLATE IX.

OF THE
TUSCAN ORDER.

To draw this, or any other Order.

NAMES OF THE MOULDINGS.

In the Entablature.		In the Column.	
E a Fillet	} In the Cornice	Q Fillet	} In the Capital
F Cima Recta		R Fascia	
G Fillet		S Ovolo	
H Corona		T Fillet	
I Ovolo		U Neck of the Capital	
K Fillet			
L Cavetto			
M ———	Frize	V Bead	} In the Shaft
		W Fillet	
N Tenia	} In the Architrave	X Fillet	} In the Base
O Upper Fascia		Y Torus	
P Lower Fascia		Z Plinth	

Make a scale of the diameter of the column at the bottom; first divide it into six equal parts called modules, divide the first of these into ten, which are called minutes; then every member of the order is so many minutes of this scale, either in height or projection: the operation is as follows: draw an axis or perpendicular, through the middle of the column; on this line set all your heights, or on any other line parallel to it: then make another line parallel to the axis at the distance of twenty-five minutes, which allows five minutes on each side for the diminution at top; from this line set off your projections, as figured in the plate, for example the projection of the top fillet E is forty-two minutes, and the projection of the next fillet G is thirty-two

minutes

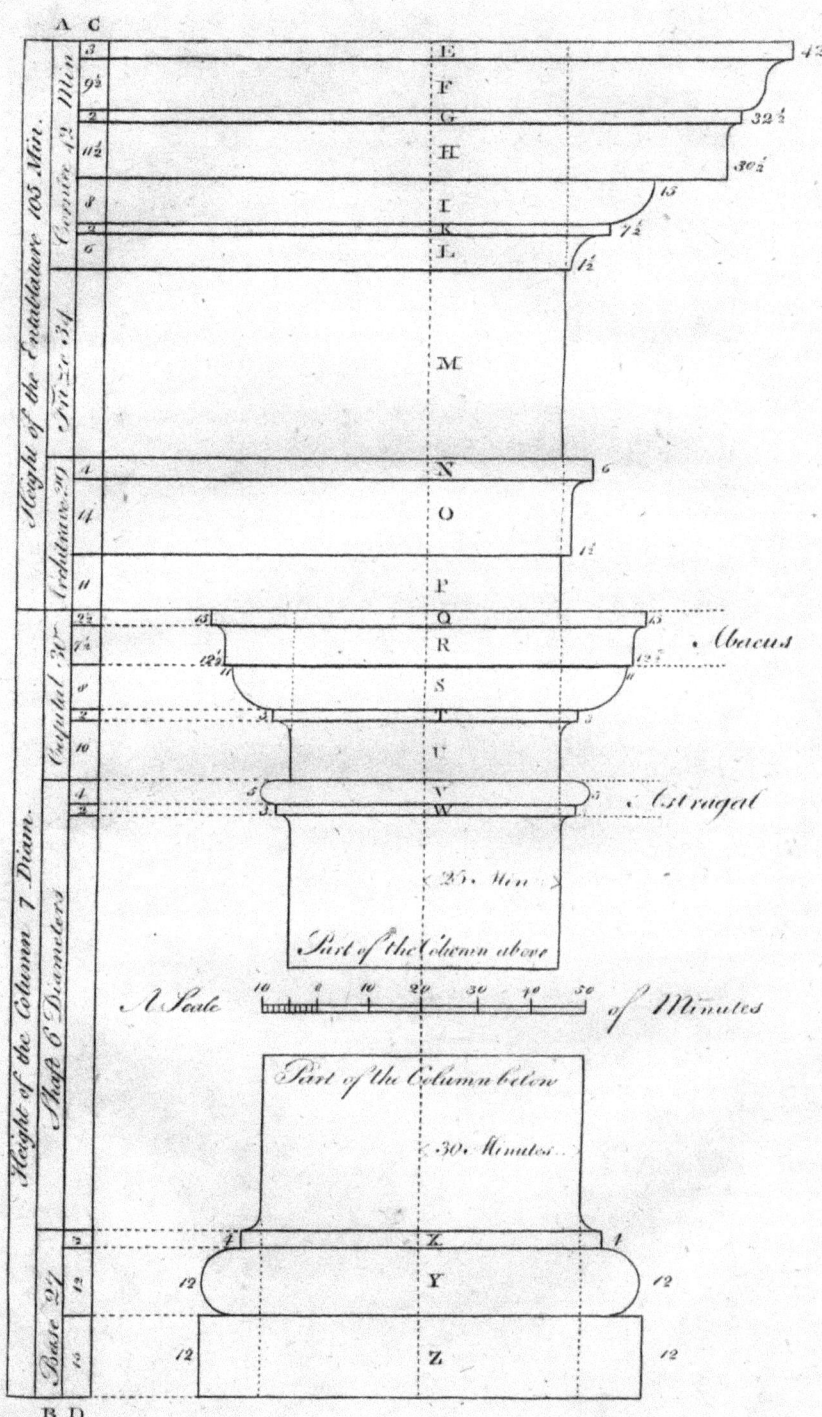

minutes and a half; then proceed to draw the cima recta, as already shewn at Plate I, and afterwards all the other members, until you come to the base which is set off from the outer extremity of the column, that is thirty minutes from the axis.

In the Tuscan order, the column is seven diameters high, that is seven times its diameter at the base, the entablature is one fourth of the height of the column: but if the order has a pedestal, which is seldom the case, it will be one-fifth part of the entire order in height.

To make this practice as easy as possible to the workman, the following examples will be found useful.

To find the diameter of the Tuscan Column, when that alone is to be executed.

RULE.

Divide the height of the column by seven, and the quotient will be the diameter.

EXAMPLE I.

Suppose it were required to execute the Tuscan Column alone, to the height of twenty-two feet, three inches, I demand the diameter of the column.

OPERATION.

$$7) \; 22 \ldots 3$$
$$\overline{3 \ldots 2\tfrac{1}{7}}$$

So that the diameter of the column is three feet two inches and one-seventh part of an inch.

Divide $3 \ldots 2\tfrac{1}{7}$ into sixty equal parts, will give a scale of minutes for proportioning the parts. The diameter, found by the following rule, in feet and inches, is always supposed to be divided into sixty equal parts, for minutes.

To find the height of the Tuscan Entablature, and the diameter of its column, the entire height of the column, and entablature being given.

RULE.

Divide the height by five, and the quotient will give the height of the entablature; subtract the height of the entablature last found, from the entire height, and the remainder will be the height of the column; divide this remainder by seven, as before; and the quotient will be the diameter of the column.

EXAMPLE II.

Suppose it were required to execute the Tuscan Columns with its entablature, to the height of twenty-two feet, one inch, I demand the height of the entablature, and the diameter of the column.

OPERATION.

5) 22 .. 1
_____

    4 .. 5   height of the Entablature
_____

7) 17 .. 8   height of Column
_____

    2 .. 6$\frac{2}{7}$ diameter of the Column

The diameter of the column being now found, it will be readily put in as follows: Suppose it were required to execute a column to two feet six inches, and two-seventh parts of an inch; take a rod of that dimension, and divide it into six equal parts, or modules, and the first part again into ten for minutes, and proceed in practice in the same manner as if you were drawing it on paper.

To find the diameter of the Column, the height of the Entablature, and the height of the Pedestal, when the whole is to be executed to a given height.

RULE.

Divide the entire height by five, and the quotient will be the height of the pedestal: subtract this height from the entire height, and the remainder will be the height of the column, with its entablature: divide the remainder again by five, and the quotient will be the height of the entablature: subtract the quotient from the first remainder, and the last remainder will be the height of the column: and this last remainder being divided by seven, will give the diameter of the column.

Example.

It is required to execute the Tuscan Order compleat, with an entablature, column, and pedestal, to the height of thirty feet: I demand the height of the pedestal, height of the entablature, and diameter of the column.

Operation.

5) 30

6 feet, the height of the Pedestal

5) 24 height of the Column and Entablature

4 .. 9⅕ height of the Entablature

7) 19 .. 2⅘ height of the Column

2 .. 8⅗ diameter of the Column

D   PLATE

PLATE X.

The Tuscan Order properly shaded is given as an example, after the manner of setting out the parts, and striking the mouldings are well acquired.

PLATE XI.

TO DRAW THE TUSCAN COLUMN TO A GIVEN HEIGHT.

For the Column.

Fig. 1. Divide the height in seven equal parts, one of these is the diameter of the column, and a scale to proportion the parts by. See Page 16.

For the Column and Entablature.

Fig. 2. Divide the given height into five equal parts, give one for the height of the entablature; then divide the remaining four into seven parts, of which one will be the diameter of the column.

For the Column and Entablature upon a Subplinth.

Divide the whole height C D into twelve equal parts, one will be the height of the subplinth; divide the remaining eleven into five equal parts, one will be the height of the entablature; divide the remaining four of these parts into seven, and one will be the diameter of the column.

For

Tuscan Order

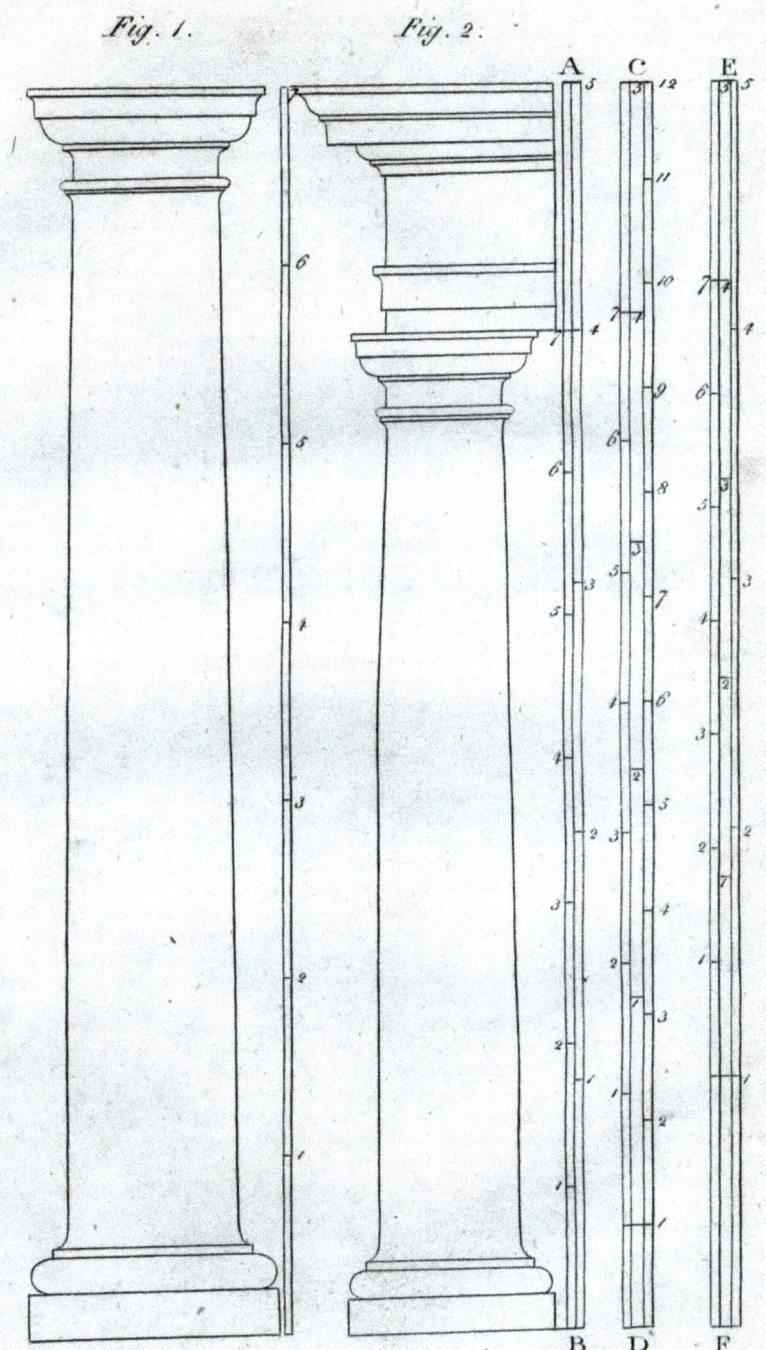

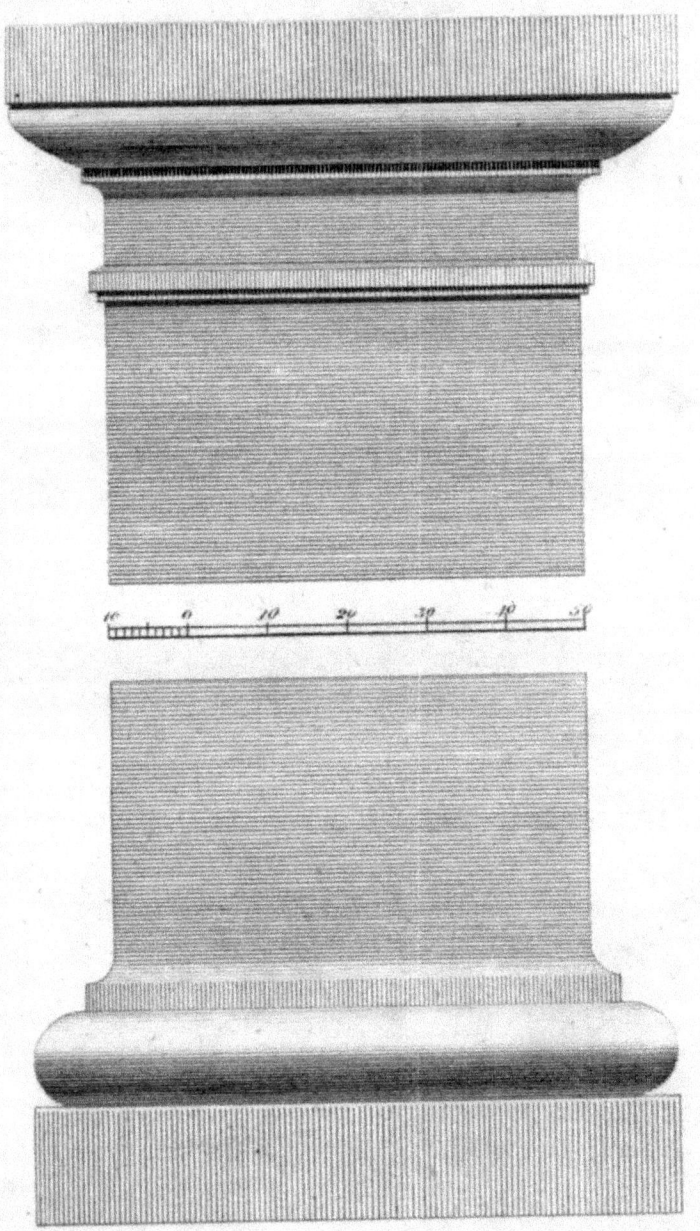

A finished Base and Capital for a pilaster

Drawn by P. Nicholson. Engraved by Roberts.

For the Column and Entablature upon a Pedestal.

Divide the whole height E F into five equal parts, the lower one will give the height of the pedestal; divide the remaining four into five equal parts, the upper one will give the height of the entablature; divide the remaining four of these into seven equal parts, and one is the diameter of the column.

PLATE XII.

Is a Tuscan base and capital for a pilaster, the scale will shew the proportions of the parts.

PLATE XIII.

OF THE DORIC ORDER.

THE manner of drawing the parts of the Doric Order is much the same as in the Tuscan; the heights and projection of the parts being taken from the diameter of the column at bottom, which is a scale, alike in all the orders; so that the drawing and executing of the Tuscan order if well understood, to draw the Doric or any other order will easily be comprehended, without further instruction or repetition. One thing may seem difficult in this order, which are the Triglyphs; these in modern buildings are placed exactly over the center of the column, thirty-minutes wide, so that fifteen minutes are on each side of the axis of the column; the mutules in the cornice are exactly over them, of the same breadth; the small conical frustrum under the triglyphs are called Guttæ or bells; the manner of drawing the triglyph and bells is as follows; divide the breadth into twelve equal parts, give one to each half channel on the outside: two for each space or interval, and two for each channel, and one space will remain in the middle; every two divisions or parts is the width of a bell; the side of every bell, if continued, would terminate in a point at the top of the fillet above them; the spaces between the triglyphs, called Metopes, are generally square, and sometimes enriched with ox heads, as in Plate 15, and sometimes with pateras, according to fancy; when the column is fluted it has

twenty

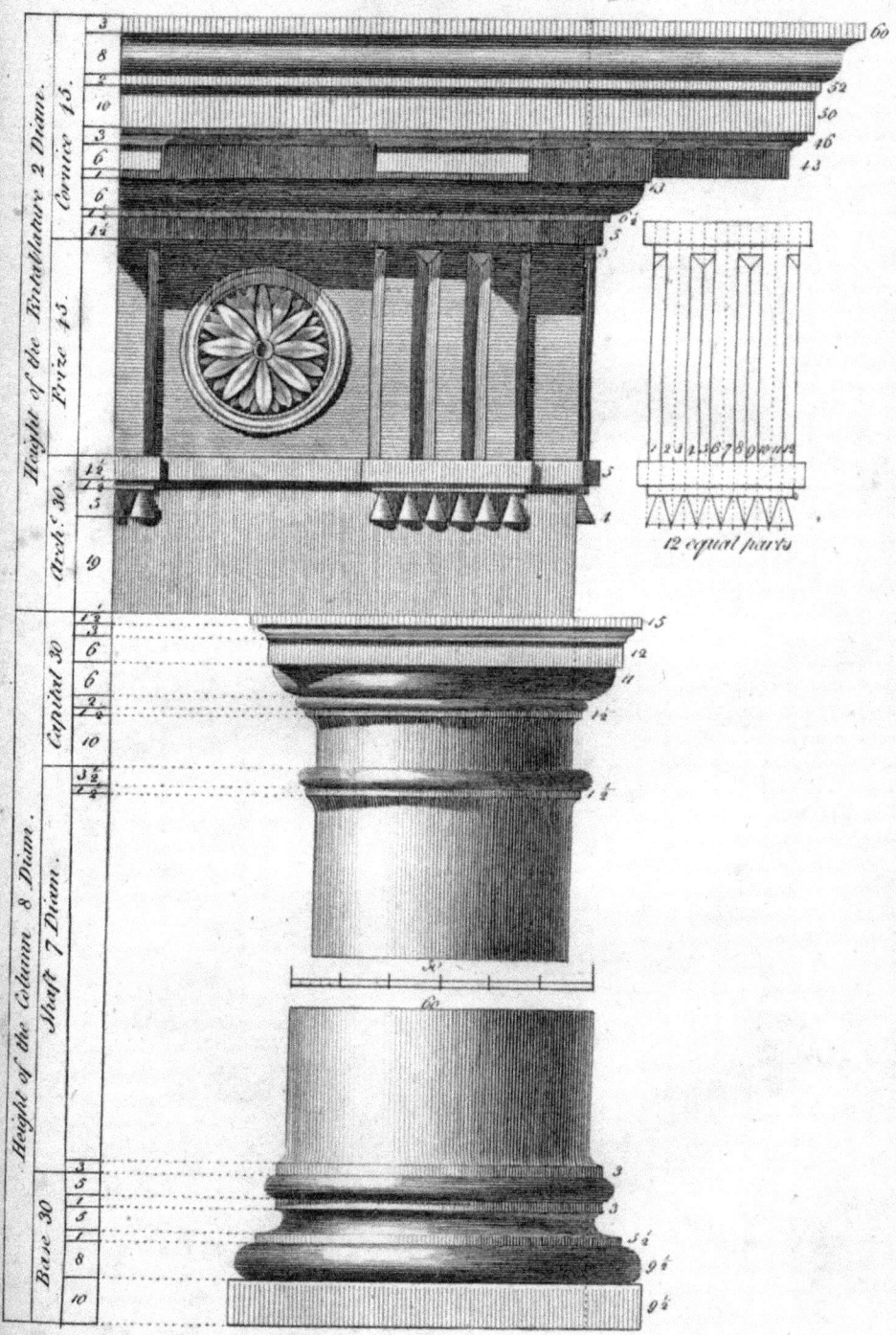

Planceer of the Doric Order.

The Doric Order with dentils.

twenty in number, and these without fillets, as in Plate 15. For the manner of drawing the flutes of the Doric column, see Plate 5; *Fig.* 1 and 2.

PLATE XIV.

Is a Doric cornice with the planceer inverted, so that the whole of the work and ornaments under the cornice may be clearly seen.

PLATE XV.

Is another example of the Doric order, with dentils in the cornice, and is very proper for the inside of a building, the column being fluted, and the whole much enriched.

This example is after the manner of the Doric order, in the theatre of Marcellus at Rome.

TO DRAW THE DORIC ORDER TO A GIVEN HEIGHT.

For the Column.

Divide the height into eight equal parts, one of the parts is the diameter of the column, which diameter is to be divided into modules and minutes, as before directed, for practice.

For the Column and Entablature,

Divide the given height into five equal parts, and the upper parts will give the height of the entablature; divide the remaining four into eight equal parts, and one will give the diameter of the column.

For

For the Column and Entablature upon a subplinth.

Divide the given height into twelve equal parts, the lower one will give the height of the subplinth, divide the remaining eleven into five equal parts, the upper one is the height of the entablature; divide the remaining four parts into eight, and one of these is the diameter of the column.

For the Column and Entablature upon a pedestal.

Divide the given height into five equal parts, the lower one is the height of the pedestal; divide the remaining four into five equal parts, and the upper one is the height of the entablature; divide the remaining four of these into eight equal parts, and one will give the diameter of the column.

PLATE XVI.

FROM THE TEMPLE OF MINERVA AT ATHENS.

Shews the profile of the order, elevation of the parts, and proportion of the members. This example is taken from the flank of the Temple, and is well adapted to all buildings, which require a solemn and dignified character. The temple from which this example is taken, is one of the numerous buildings which were erected during the administration of Pericles at Athens; he employed Calicrates, and Ictinus, as architects under Phidias. It exceeds all the remains of antiquity, in grandeur, and boldness of parts. The taste of the members of this example, is much the same as in the temple of Theseus, as will be shewn hereafter, the parts here being only of a bolder character.

Note, *The measurements are in modules and minutes.*

PLATE

Grecian Doric — Temple of Minerva. Pl. 16.

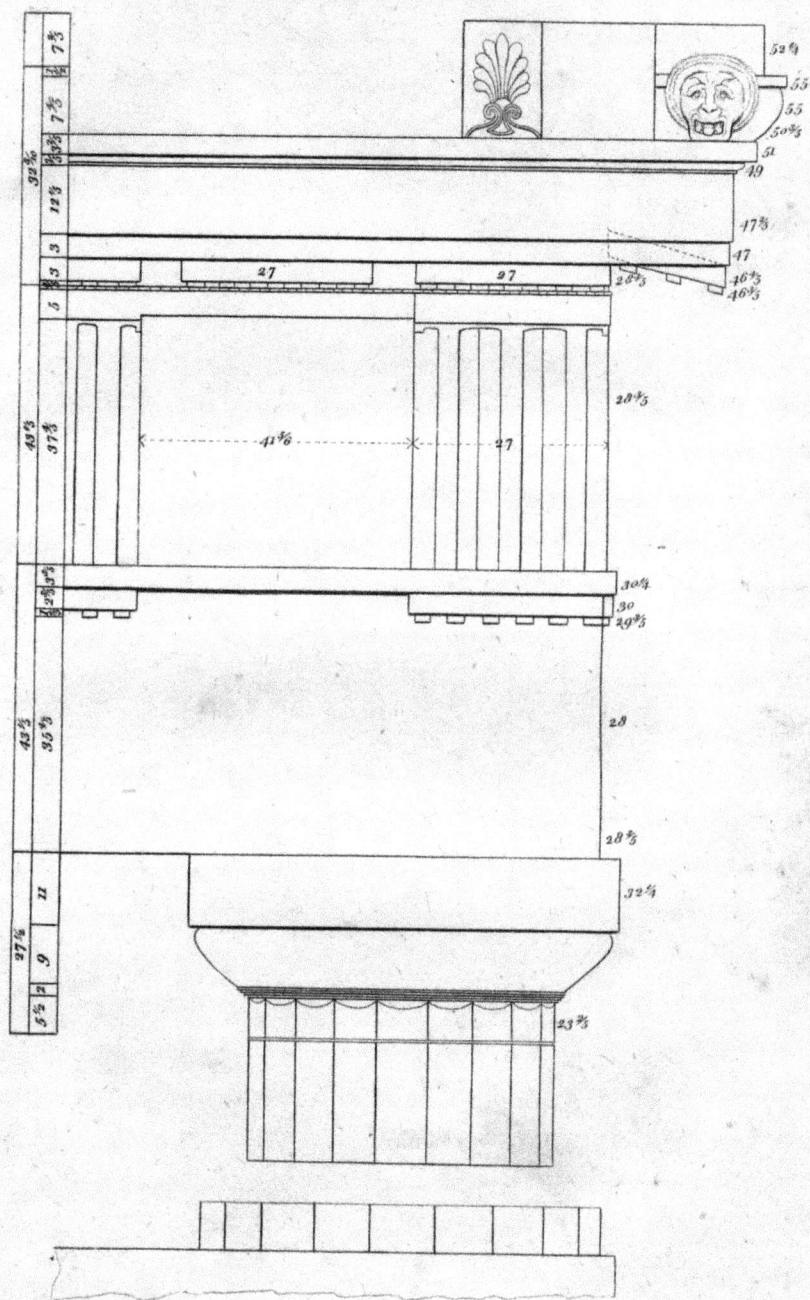

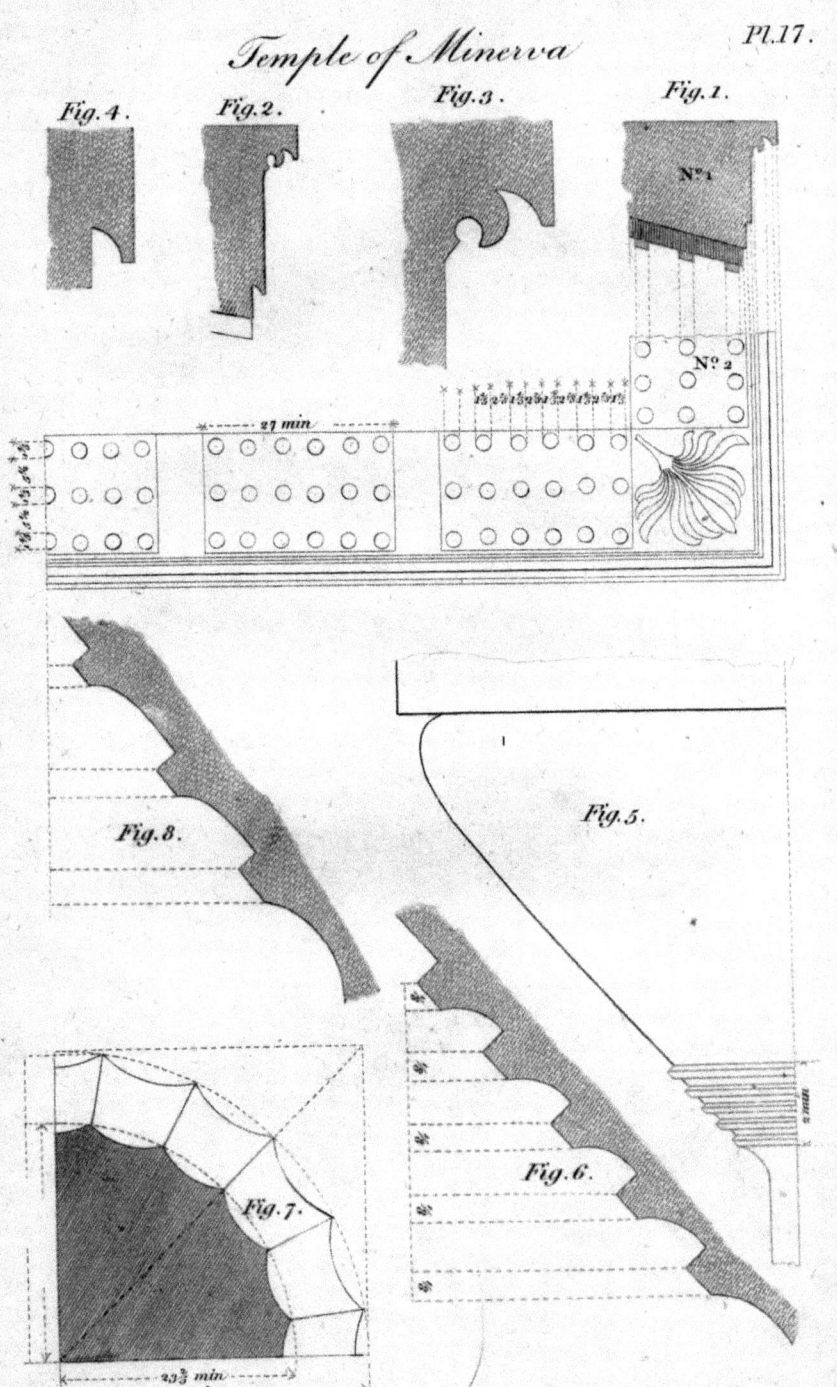

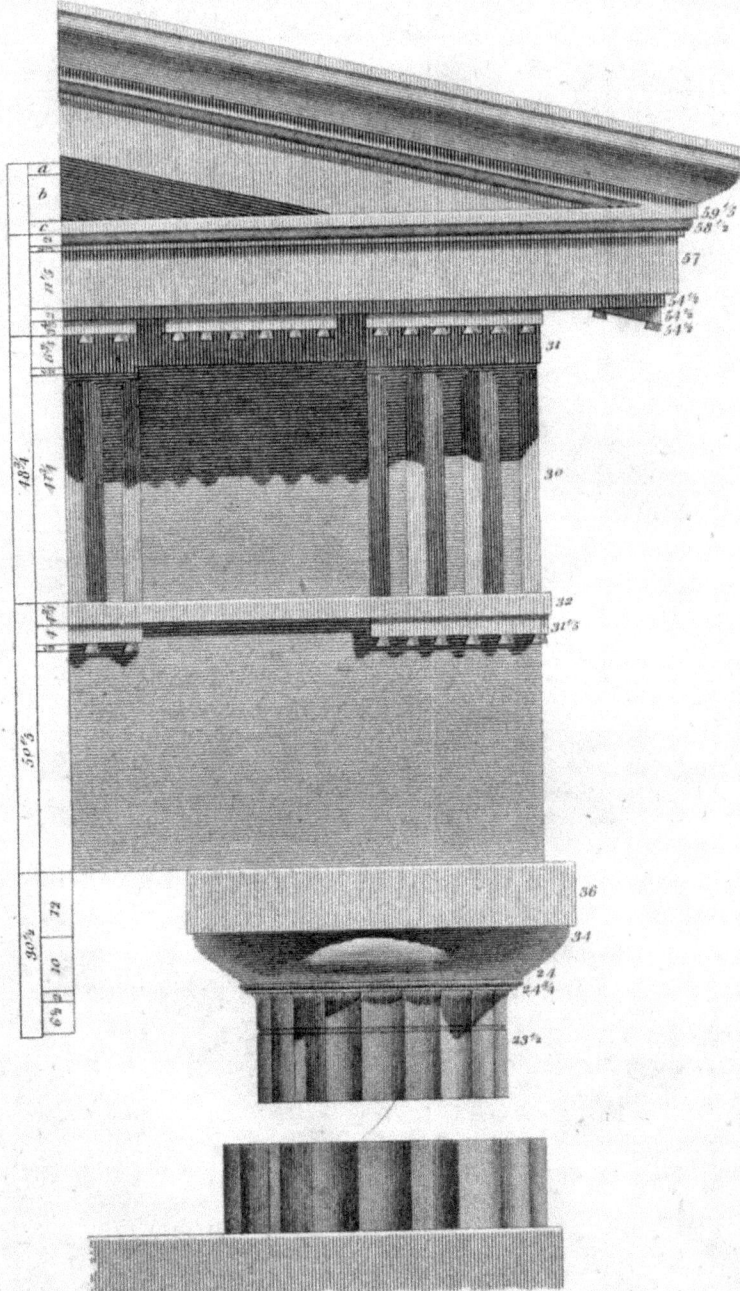

Pl. 18.

Grecian Doric — Temple of Theseus.

P. Nicholson del.   London Published by J. Taylor N.º 59 High Holborn.   J. Dadley sculp.

PLATE XVII.

PARTS AT LARGE AND IN DETAIL OF THE PRECEDING EXAMPLE.

Fig. 1. Cornice, No. 1. shews the profile, No. 2. the soffit.

Fig. 2. Profile of the front part to a larger scale.

Fig. 3. The moulding under the fillet still larger, shewing its particular form.

Fig. 4. Shews the recess or cutting upwards, in the under face of the corona.

Fig. 5. Echinus of the Capital.

Fig. 6 Annulets of the same.

Fig. 7. Quarter plan of the column at each extremity.

Fig. 8. Annulets of the interior columns.

PLATE XVIII.

FROM THE TEMPLE OF THESEUS AT ATHENS.

The building from which this example is taken is one of the most perfect remains of antiquity, and is generally supposed to be of the age of Pericles. The various parts have an elegant contour, are well proportioned, of a light character, consequently it is well adapted for private buildings. The column in the original is nearly six diameters in height. In this plate part of the pediment is shewn.

PLATE

PLATE XIX.

PARTS AT LARGE AND IN DETAIL OF THE PRECEDING EXAMPLE.

Fig. 1. Quarter plan of the column, at the superior and inferior diameter of the shaft.

Fig. 2. Profile of the cornice to a large scale.

Fig. 3. Soffit of the corona, with a section of the angular triglyph.

Fig. 4. One of the flutes shewing its proportions, and the manner of drawing its elliptical segmental figure: first draw the chord to its extent and bisect it by a perpendicular, set the depth of the flute on the perpendicular from one side of the chord, which will give the extremity of the flute: from this extremity set the radius in the contrary direction extending over the chord, which will give the centre: divide the chord of the flute into five equal parts, through the first division from each end and from the centre, draw two right lines, then upon the centre with the radius describe an arc limited by these lines, and this will give the middle part of the flute; divide each of these radial lines into three equal parts; take the first point of division in each next to the arc, and describe each remaining part of the flute, and this will form the elliptic segmental figure of the flute.

Fig. 6. Lower part of the triglyph with the architrave band, the tenia, and the pending guttæ.

PLATE

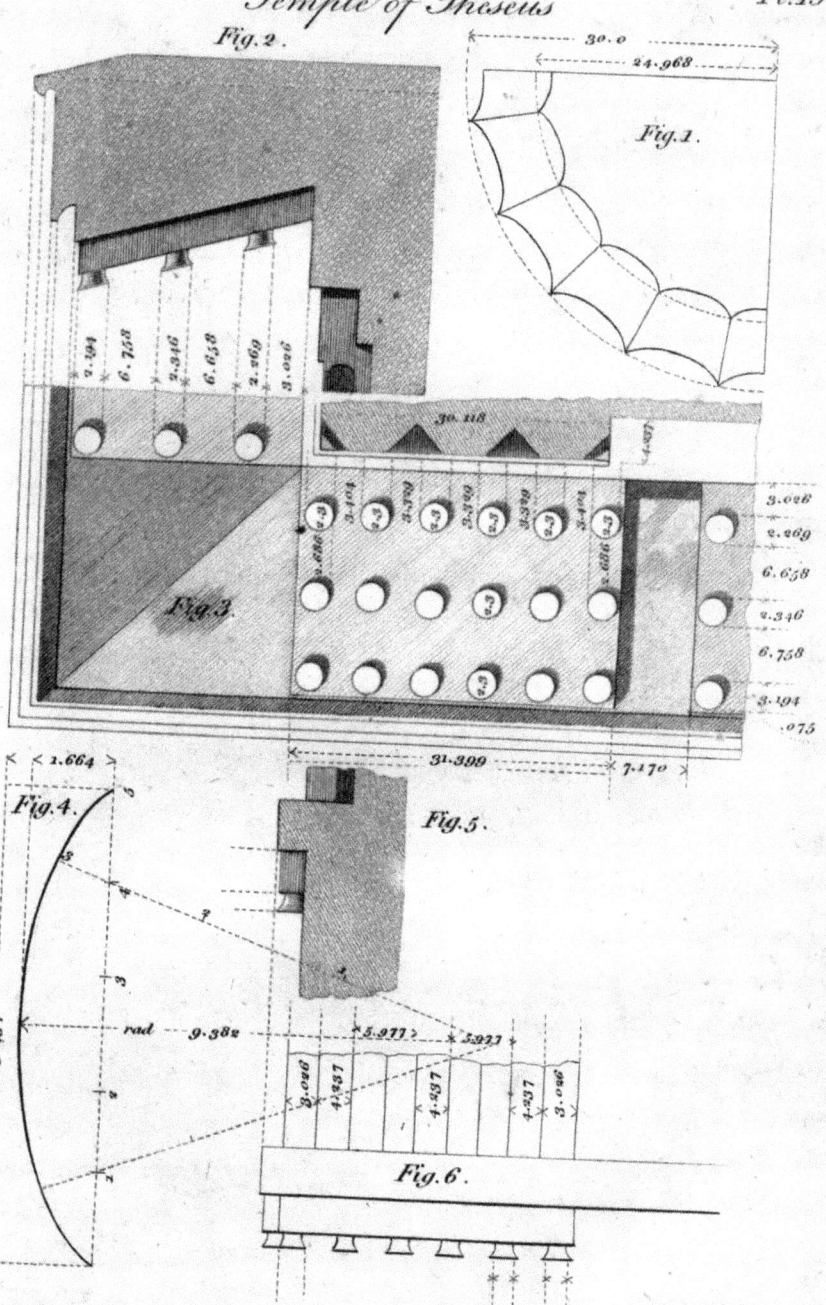

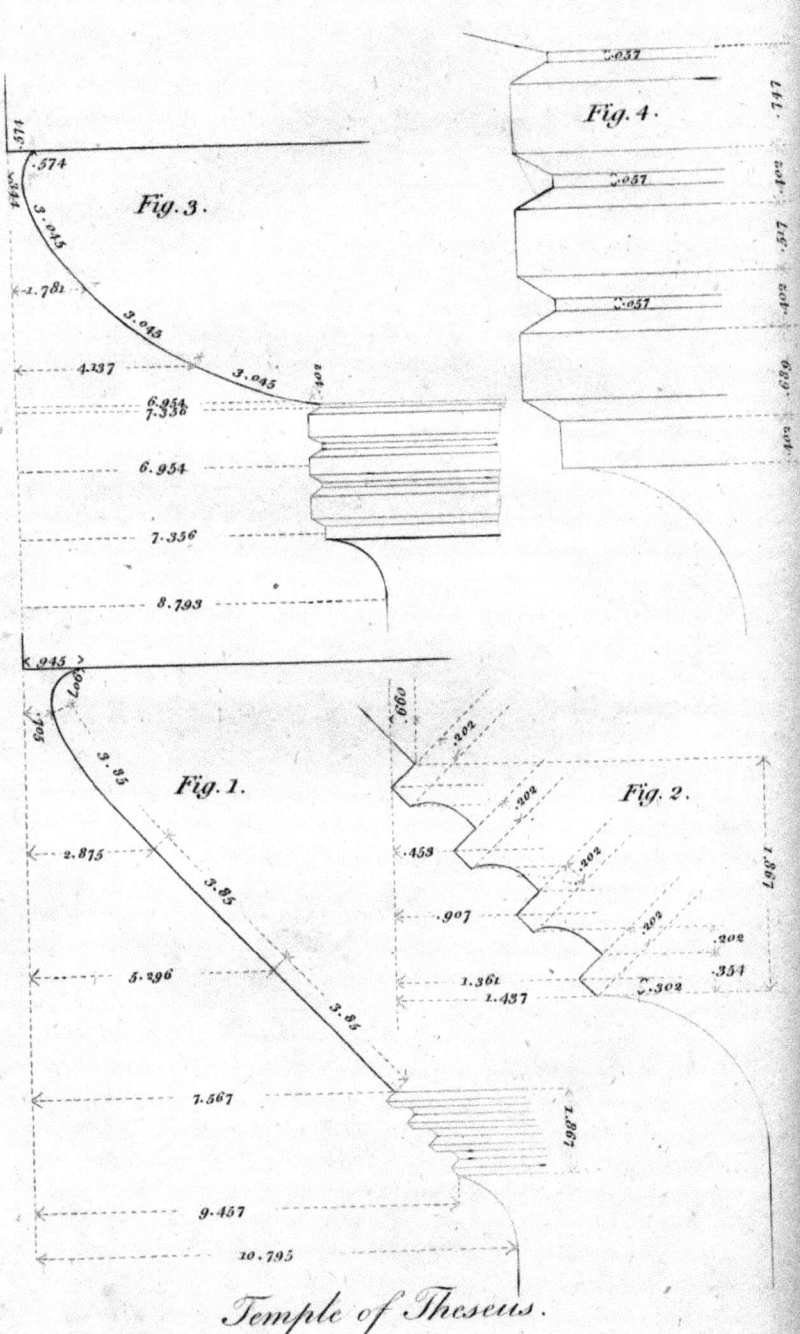

Pl. 20.

Doric Portico.

Temple of Theseus.

PLATE XX.

OTHER PARTS AT LARGE OF THE FOREGOING, AND OF THE FOLLOWING EXAMPLES.

Fig. 1. Profile of the echinus of the capital of the temple of Theseus to a large scale: this moulding as well as that of the temple of Minerva is an hyperbola, or the portion of one: the lower part from the greatest projection at top down to the bottom, being one of the legs; the upper part forming the quirk or recess above, part of the other leg, and the greatest projection the vertex. It is something singular that the very ancient mouldings in Grecian capitals should be of this form, and some of them quite straight, from one end to the other, which may be considered as a section of the cone through the vertex.

Fig. 2. Annulets under the echinus of the capital of the column. The reader may here observe that the annulets continue in the general form of the curve, *viz.* the recesses in the curve itself, and the extremities in a line parallel to that curve.

Fig. 3. Profile of the echinus of the capital of the *Doric Portico*, as in the following plate, this moulding is singular, being of an elliptical figure; it is more than a quadrant. This portico was built while the government of Athens was in the hands of the Romans, who were partial to mouldings of a uniform and bold curvature; the taste of the Grecians, it appears began to blend with that of their conquerors, hence I account for the elliptic form of this member; it is a medium between an hyperbolical and a circular moulding.

Fig. 4. Part of the annulets of the capital of the same column, no less singular in their construction than the echinus, or other members of this example, being disposed vertically, and in the form of champhered rustics; whereas the annulets of other Grecian remains follow the contour of the echinus, as has been before observed.

PLATE XXI.

FROM THE DORIC PORTICO AT ATHENS.

This plate exhibits the contour, the elevation, and proportions of the members in minutes and parts of a minute—This example although singular on account of its approach to the Roman style in the members, is, in its general form the same as other Grecian examples.

As Mr. Stuart appears to have bestowed particular attention to the measures of these Doric examples, here shewn, I have, with considerable pains reduced the original measures of feet, inches, and decimals of an inch, by arithmetical calculations into minutes, and decimal parts of a minute, and not by measuring them from two scales which would have been more expeditious to me, but much less accurate: each minute is consequently divided into ten equal parts, each of these again into ten, and so on as long as division can be made—By these universal proportions, the construction will be more easily obtained by students in general.

OF

Grecian Doric — Portico at Athens. Pl. 21.

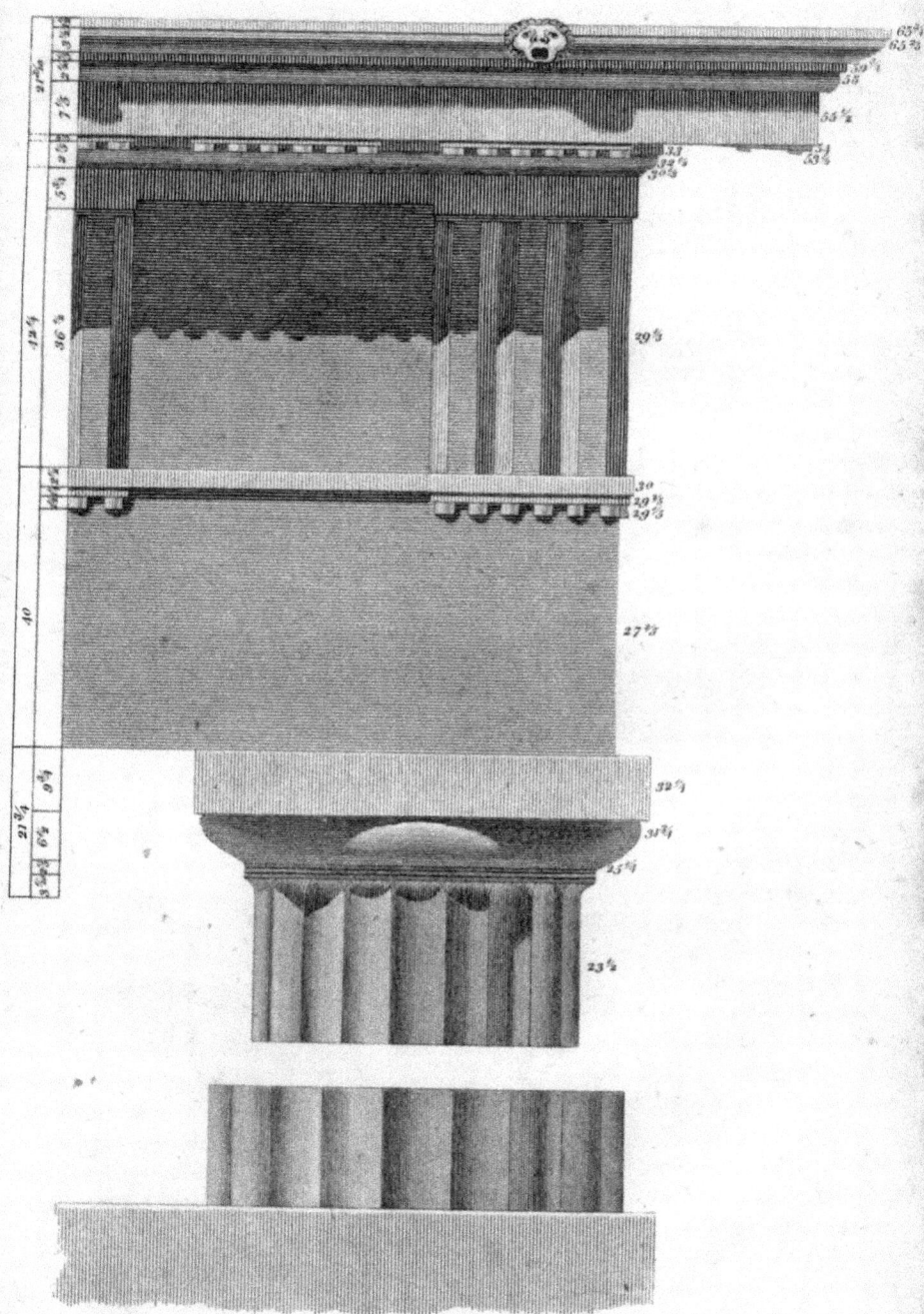

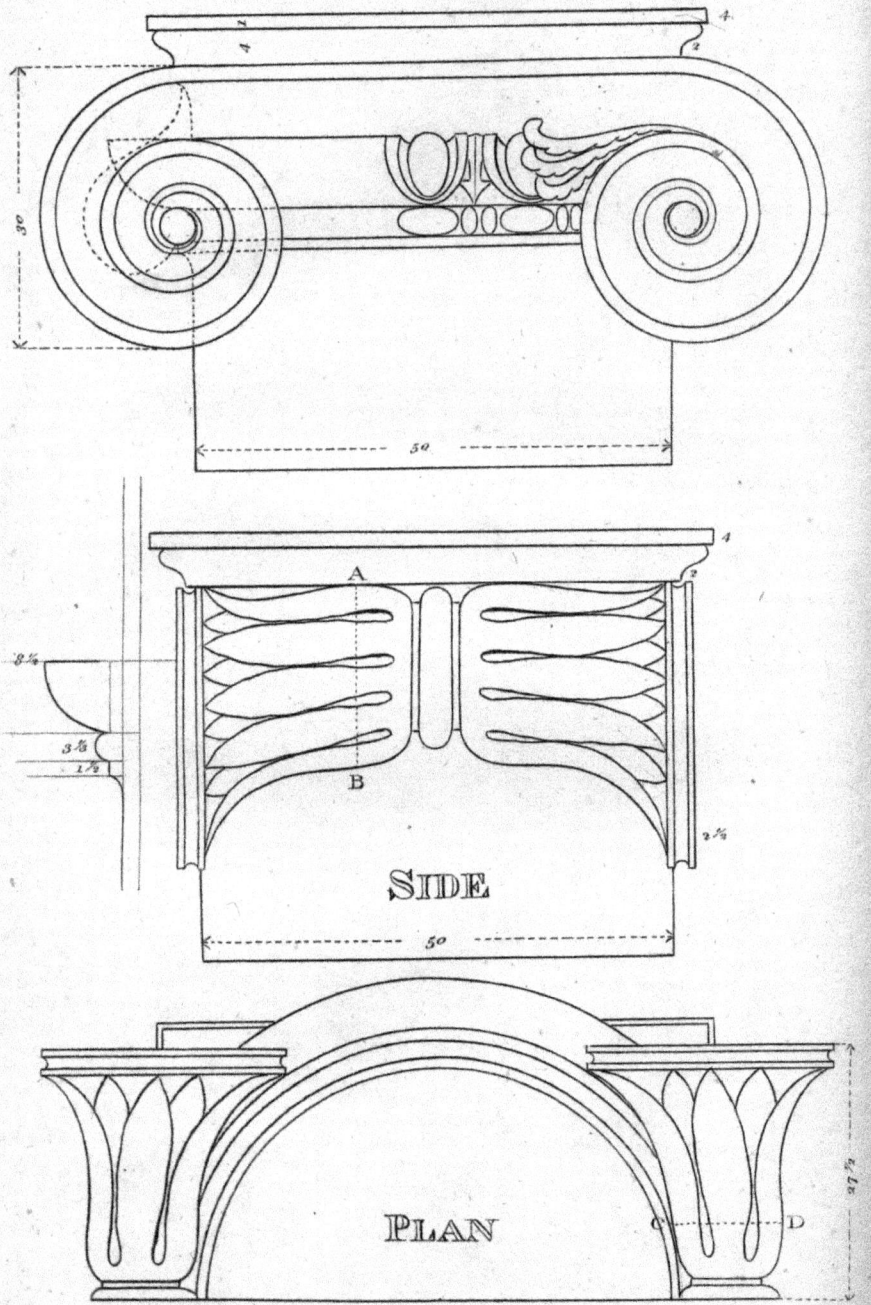

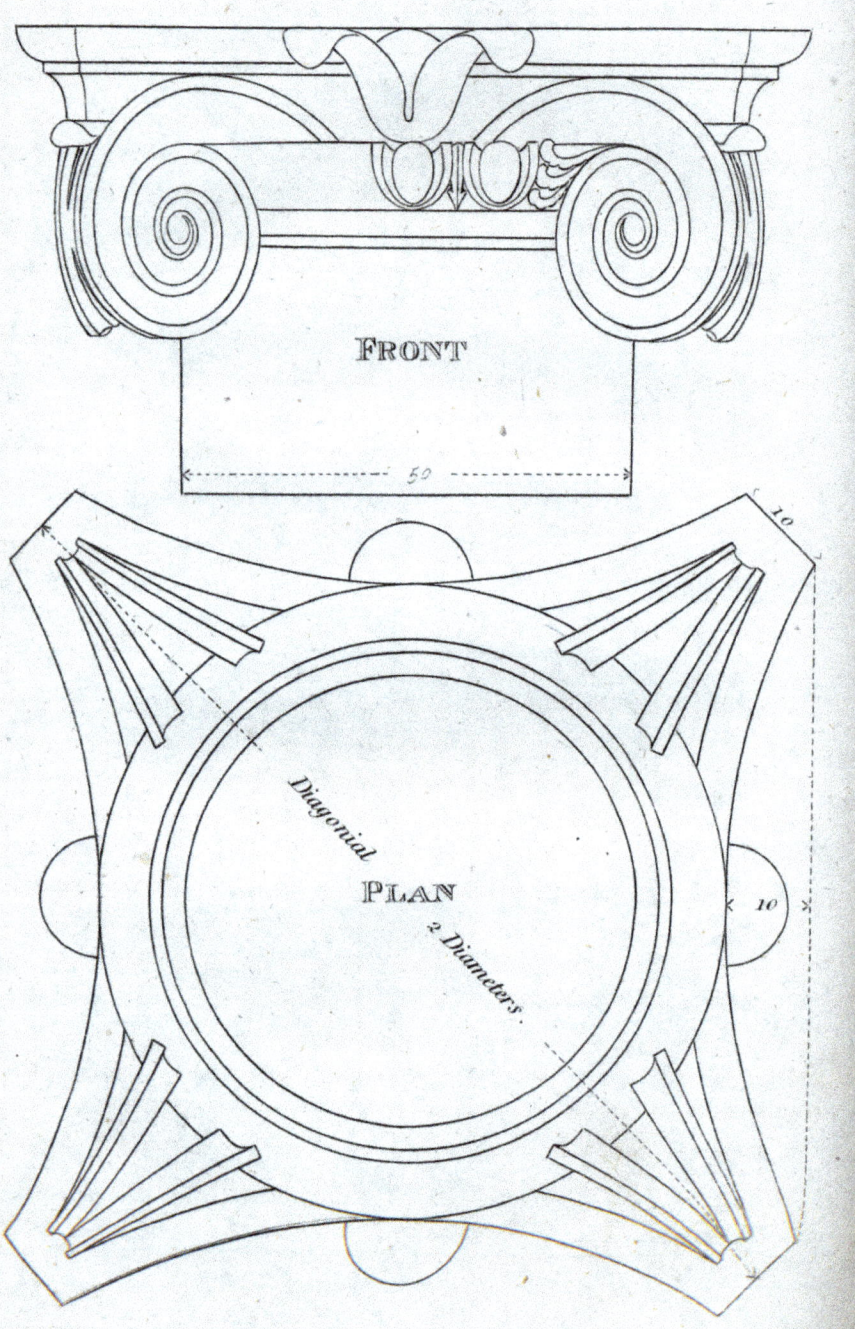

OF THE IONIC ORDER.

PLATE XXII.

Shews the front, side and plan of the *Roman Ionic* capital. The whole height of the volute is twenty-eight minutes, the center of the volute is sixteen minutes from the top side of the list; and is described as in Plate 28; the bead, or upper part of the astragal is equal in thickness and in height, to the eye of the volute; the height of the ovolo above, is from the upper side of the eye, to the upper side of the list in the second revolution; the projection of the cincture, or hollow under the fillet of the astragal, is equal to the height of the fillet; and the projection of the bead is a semicircle; for the ovolo, the quarter of a circle, whose projection is from the perpendicular line of the fillet. The dotted line upon the volute, is a section through the side at A B; or through the plan at C D; the ornamental part is drawn by hand.

PLATE XXIII.

The front and plan of the angular Ionic capital; the plan is inverted, that the mouldings underneath the abacus may be seen; the volutes in front are drawn according to Plate 29; this sort of capital has an advantage over the others, it fronts each of its sides alike;

alike; which is not the case with the Grecian capital, unless one of the angles is horned at the return of the building; which is unpleasing to some, and not considered as correct.

PLATE XXIV.

Is the Ionic order with dentils in the cornice on an attic base; the capital is in the Grecian taste; the manner of drawing the upper list is the same as described to Plate 28, the under list is drawn by hand, the other parts are obvious to inspection.

PLATE XXV.

The Ionic order with modillions, and an angular capital; the measures of the parts are accurately figured; *Fig.* 1. is a section of the capital through the middle of the abacus, in order to shew the projection of the mouldings.

TO DRAW THE IONIC ORDER TO A GIVEN HEIGHT.
For the Column and Entablature.

Divide the whole height into six equal parts, give the upper one to the entablature, divide the lower five into nine parts, and one will give the diameter of the column, to be divided into sixty minutes as a scale to work, or draw by.

For the Column and Entablature on a subplinth.

Divide the whole height into twelve equal parts, give the lower one to the subplinth, and proceed with the remaining eleven as above, and you will get the height of the entablature, and the diameter of the column.

For

Pl. 24

Ionic Order

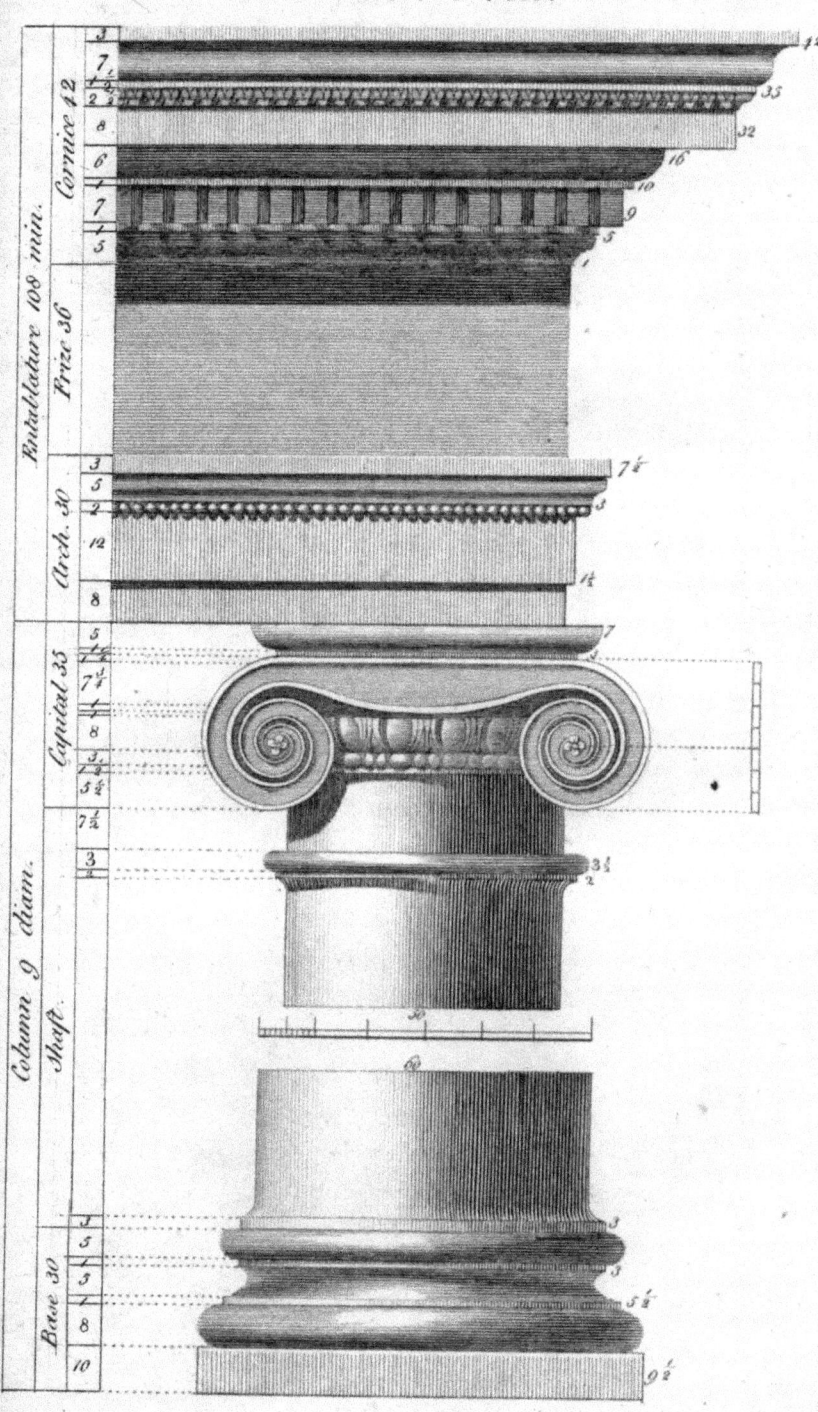

Modern Ionic

Plancere of the Ionic Order.

London, Published by I & J Taylor, N.° 56 High Holborn.

Ionic Temple at Athens. Pl. 27.

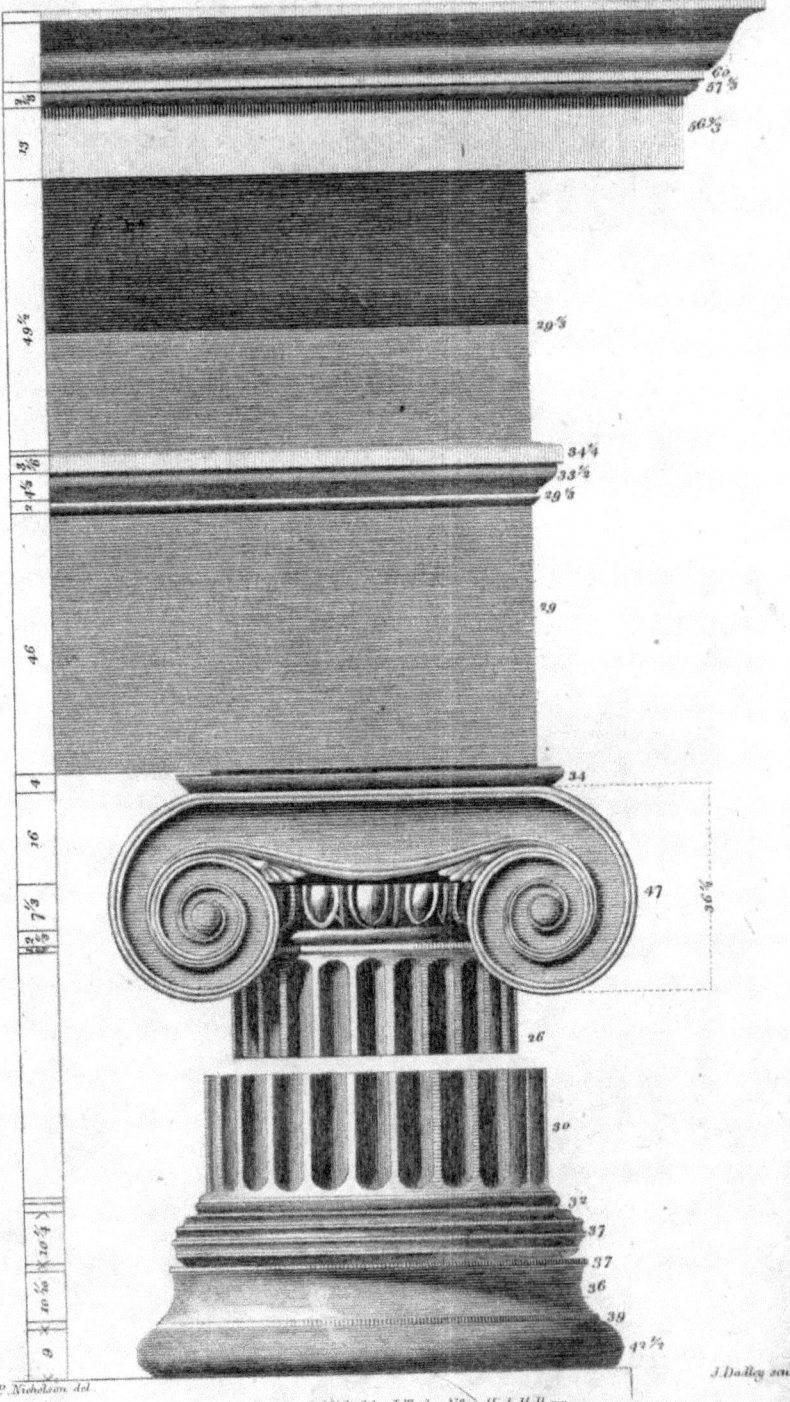

P. Nicholson del.
London: Published by J. Taylor, N.º 59 High Holborn.
J. Dadley sculp.

For the Column Entablature and Pedestal.

The height of the pedestal, for this or any of the five orders, is always one fifth part of the entire height, then the height of the entablature, and diameter of the column, is found as before.

PLATE XXVI.

The Ionic cornice with the planceer inverted, shewing the finishings underneath the cornice.

PLATE XXVII.

FROM THE IONIC TEMPLE ON THE ILISSUS, AT ATHENS.

This is a very fine example, uniting elegance with simplicity: the column is well proportioned in all its parts; the turnings of the spirals are gracefully formed, and the volutes which form the capital are bold, which give an appearance truly characteristic of this order. The members of the entablature are few, but their effect is clear and distinct calculated for effect at a distance.

PLATE XXVIII.

TO DESCRIBE THE IONIC VOLUTE.

Divide the height P Q into seven equal parts, upon the third division describe a circle about C as a center, whose diameter will be equal to one of the parts; draw the square V W X U, and in that square draw another, whose angles shall touch the sides of the former square in the middle. In order to make the construction of the centers appear plain, the center part is shewn above of a larger size, and the same letters of reference put to each; divide C 1 and C 2 each into three equal parts at 9, 5; 10, and 6; divide C 10 into two equal parts at x, if the volute is intended to be on the right hand, as in this example; but if on the left, divide C 9 into two equal parts, and proceed in each case as follows: from x draw the perpendicular line, cutting the side S F of the square at D; from D make D E and D F equal to G 1 or G 2; join E H and F H, draw 5, 4 . . 9, 8 . . 10, 11, and 6, 7, parallel to the perpendicular side of the square, cutting E H, and F H, at 4, 8 . 3 . 7 . 11; then 1 . . 2 . . 3 . . 4 . . 5 . . 6 . . 7 . . 8 . . 9 . . 10 . . 11 . . and 12 are the centers. Begin at 1, and with the radius 1 A, describe the quadrant A B, of the volute; on 2, with the radius 2 B, describe the quadrant B C; on 3, describe the quadrant C D; proceed in this manner with all the quadrants, till you touch the eye at U, and it will compleat one side of the fillet.

Ionic Volute.

Pl. 28.

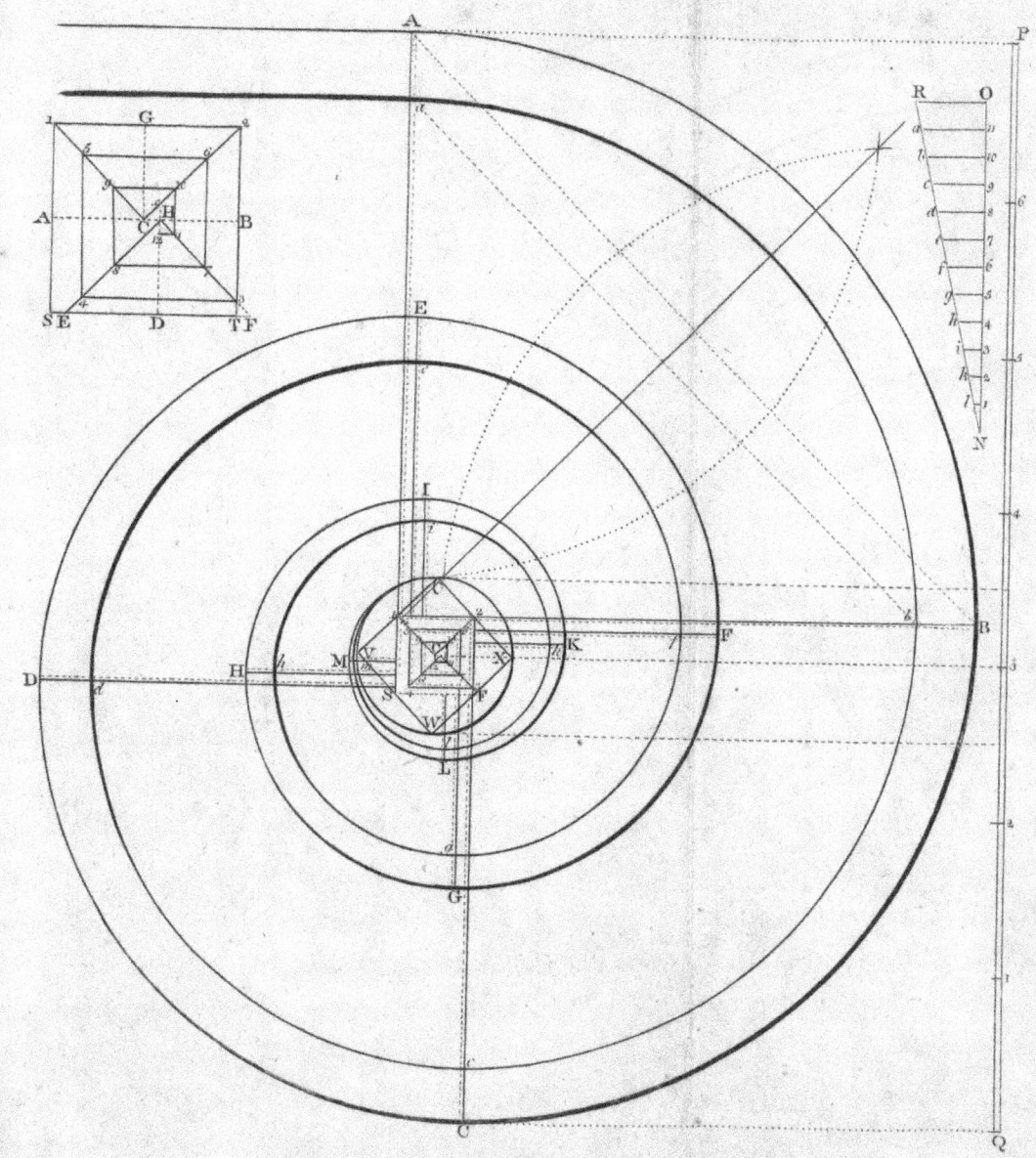

TO DRAW THE INSIDE OF THE FILLET.

Divide the thickness of the list A *a* at the top into twelve equal parts, by means of the scale N, O, R, as follows; begin at N, and with any opening of the compass run it twelve times from N to O; draw O R, making any angle with O N; make O R equal the thickness of the fillet at A *a*; join R N, draw *a* 11, *b* 10, *c* 9, *d* 8, &c, parallel to R O; make the thickness of the list at B *b*, equal to *a* 11; and D *d*, equal to *b* 10, &c. at the beginning of every quadrant; join *a b* and bisect it by a perpendicular meeting the eye a little within the first center, set the same small distance within all the other centers, and proceed to describe the inside of the list, in the same manner as the outside, and it will end in a point with the outside at U; and the volute will be compleated.

PLATE XXIX.

TO DRAW AN ANGULAR VOLUTE.

Divide the perpendicular height A B, as in *Fig.* 1, into twenty-three equal parts; take the centre G, ten divisions from the bottom, or thirteen from the top, through the center G draw H I perpendicular to A B; bisect the angle B, G, I by the diagonal line D, C; through the first division K above H, on the line A B, draw K E parallel to H I, cutting the line D C at E, on G as a center, with a radius G E, describe a circle cutting D C on the opposite side of the center at F; divide F E into six equal parts at 3, 5, G, 6, 4, F, then on E as a centre with a radius E B describe an arc B C cutting D C at C, on F with a radius F C describe the semicircle C, A, K, cutting C D at K, on 3 with a distance 3 K describe a semicircle K L, on 4 as a center with the radius 4 L describe a semicircle L M, on 5 as a center with a radius 5 M describe a semicircle M N; lastly on C with a radius 6 N, describe a semicircle N E, touching the center at E, then figure I will be compleated. This method will describe an elliptical volute to a given height, but not to any given width, this is only a preparation to what follows.

TO DESCRIBE AN ELLIPTICAL VOLUTE TO ANY GIVEN HEIGHT AND PROJECTION FROM THE CENTRE.

Fig. 2. Divide the given height L M into twenty-three equal parts as before, taking the centre E ten from the bottom, or thirteen from the top, through N the first division above E draw N F, cutting the diagonal line

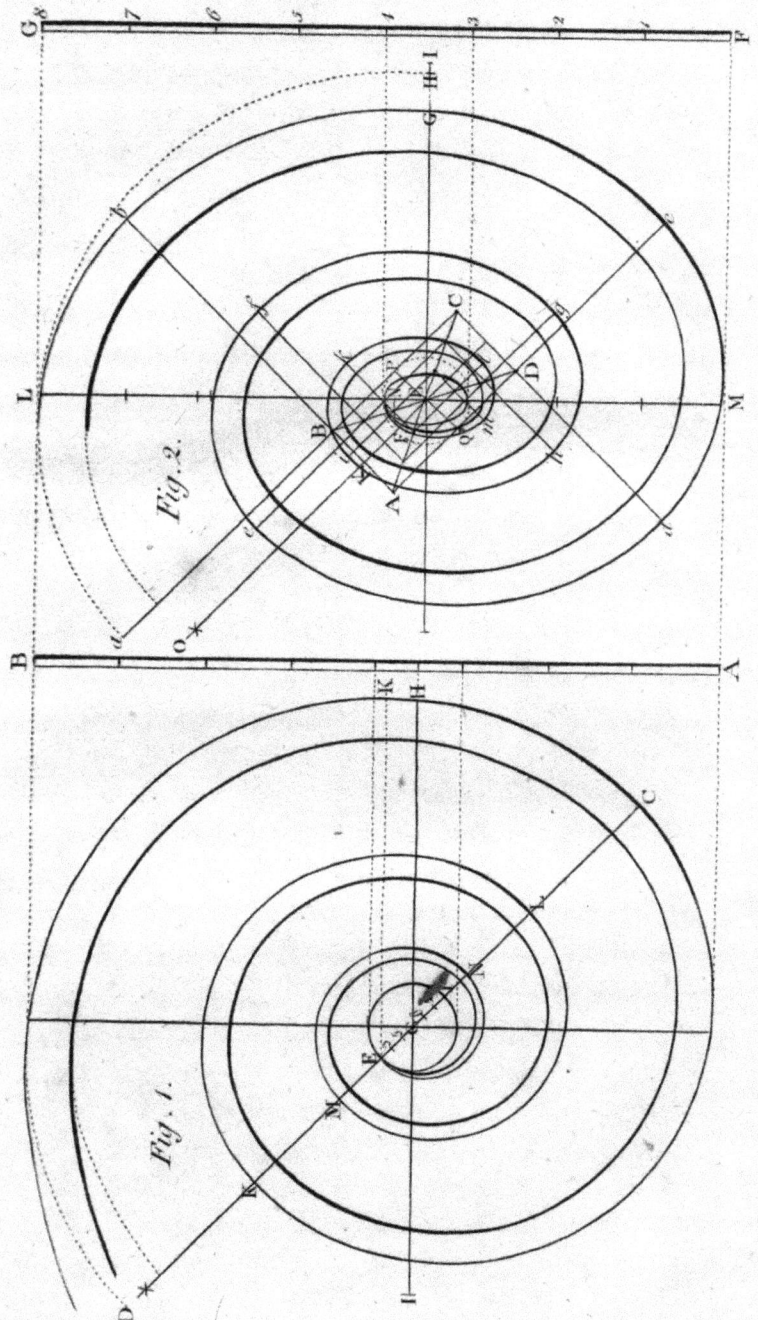

Pl. 29.

line E O at F, on E as a center with a radius E F, describe the dotted circle, or through E draw P Q at right angles to the diagonal line O E, make E P and E Q each equal E F, on F as a center with the distance L F, describe an arc L H, cutting E H at right angles to L M at H, from E make E G equal to the distance the projection of the volute is intended to be from the center, divide G H into six equal parts, and set one of the parts to I; make E K and E R each equal to the sum of the two lines E F and G I, through the points K, P, R, Q, compleat the parallelogram A B C D, whose sides A B, D C, is parallel to P Q and A D, B C parallel to K R, draw the diagonals A C and B D, and divide each of them into six equal parts, then on B as a center, with the radius B L describe the arc L b, cutting A B produced at b, on A as a center with the radius A b, describe the arc $b\,c$, cutting A D produced at c, on D as a center with the radius D c, describe an arc $c\,d$, cutting C D produced at d, on C as a center with a radius C d, describe an arc $d\,e$, on 5 as a center with a radius 5 e, describe an arc $e\,f$, on 6 as a center with the radius 6 f, describe an arc $f\,g$, on 7 as a center with the radius 7 g, describe an arc $g\,h$, on 8 as a center with the radius 8 h describe an arc $h\,i$, proceed in this manner, beginning the third revolution at 9, till you end at 12; lastly describe an ellipsis touching the last center of the third revolution E, being its center, and its transverse and conjugate axis being in the same ratio as the length or height of the volute is to its width, and it will be finished.

F   PLATE

PLATE XXX.

THE MANNER OF GLUEING UP THE IONIC CAPITAL.

Fig. 1. for a column; the parts marked B, B, &c. are triangular blocks of wood, glued upon the front, in order to compleat the angular square; then the pieces A A A, &c. are glued upon them; this is one method of glueing up the capital.

Another method is, to glue the triangular blocks C C, at the angle of the abacus; then the four sides of the abacus as D E E, may be made of one entire length, and mitered at the horns; or they may have a joint in the middle of the abacus, where the rose comes, as the workman shall think fit; this will either do for a column or pilaster.

Fig. 2. is a manner of glueing up the abacus for a pilaster capital; but in my opinion, it is far from being a compleat method, for when all the superfluous wood is worked off, the joints at the horn will be in various directions, and the end of the wood buting against the grain never holds fast.

Methods of gluing up Ionic Capitals. Pl. 30

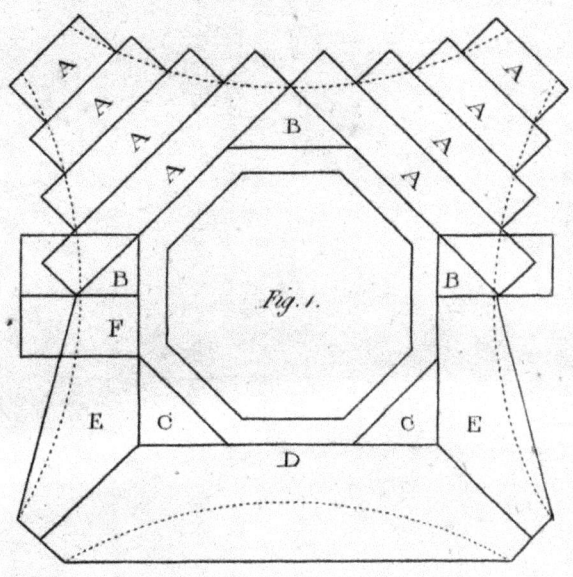

Fig. 1.

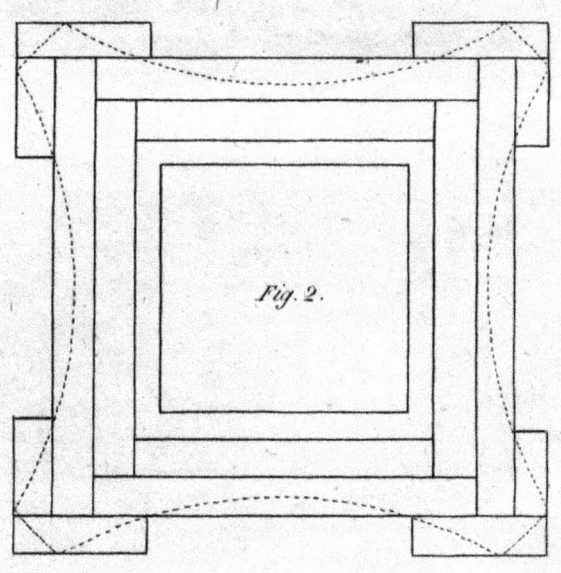

Fig. 2.

London, Published by I & J. Taylor, N° 56 High Holborn.

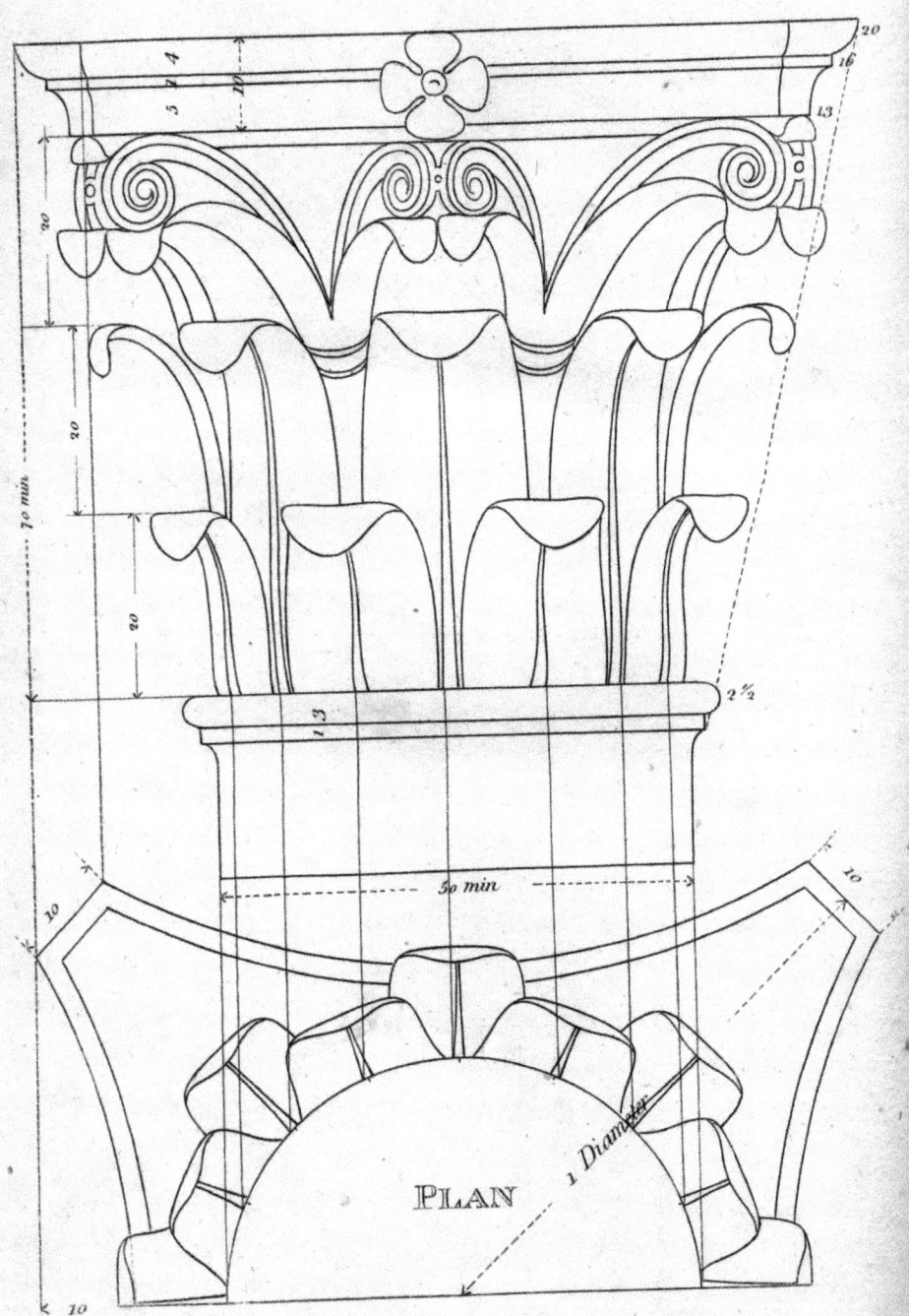

Corinthian Capital

Pl. 31.

PLAN

Pl. 32

Corinthian Order

OF THE CORINTHIAN ORDER.

PLATE XXXI.

Is the Corinthian capital and plan in outline for the sake of clearness; to find the places of the stems of the leaves, divide the semi-plan into eight equal parts, and draw the plan of the leaves, with their stems; from the side of each stem draw the perpendicular lines to the elevation of the capital, and it will give the breadth of each stem on the front, the projection of the tops of the leaves, is from a line, joining the top of the abacus, and the astragal at the bottom of the capital, the heights of the leaves are shewn in Plate 32, the out-line of the leaves are drawn by hand; observe, that these out-lines are supposed only to be in black lead pencil, preparatory to shading and finishing them, as shewn in Plate 32.

PLATE XXXII.

Is the Corinthian order fully enriched with ornaments, which may be executed with the order or not, according to the place it is intended for; before the student begins to draw this order, he ought to be well acquainted with drawing the various kinds of ornaments and foliage, otherwise he never will produce a masterly performance; or be able to make any considerable figure in drawing so elegant a subject.

PLATE XXXIII.

The Corinthian cornice, with the planceer inverted. The height and projections of the cornice are the same as in Plate 32.

PLATE XXXIV.

Is the manner of drawing the Corinthian column with an entablature entire; or the column and entablature on a pedestal; or upon a subplinth. The diameter of the column is one tenth part of its height; the height of the entablature, and pedestal, are found in the same manner as in the Ionic order; that is, the height A B, *Fig.* 1. is divided into six equal parts, the upper one is for the height of the entablature; one half of which, will of course be the diameter of the column. The rods C D, and E F, shew the methods of setting off the order when it is to be executed on a pedestal, or on a subplinth; the pedestal takes one fifth of the entire order, the subplinth one twelfth. The diameter of the column is one tenth of its height.

Plancer of the Corinthian Order

Corinthian Pl.34

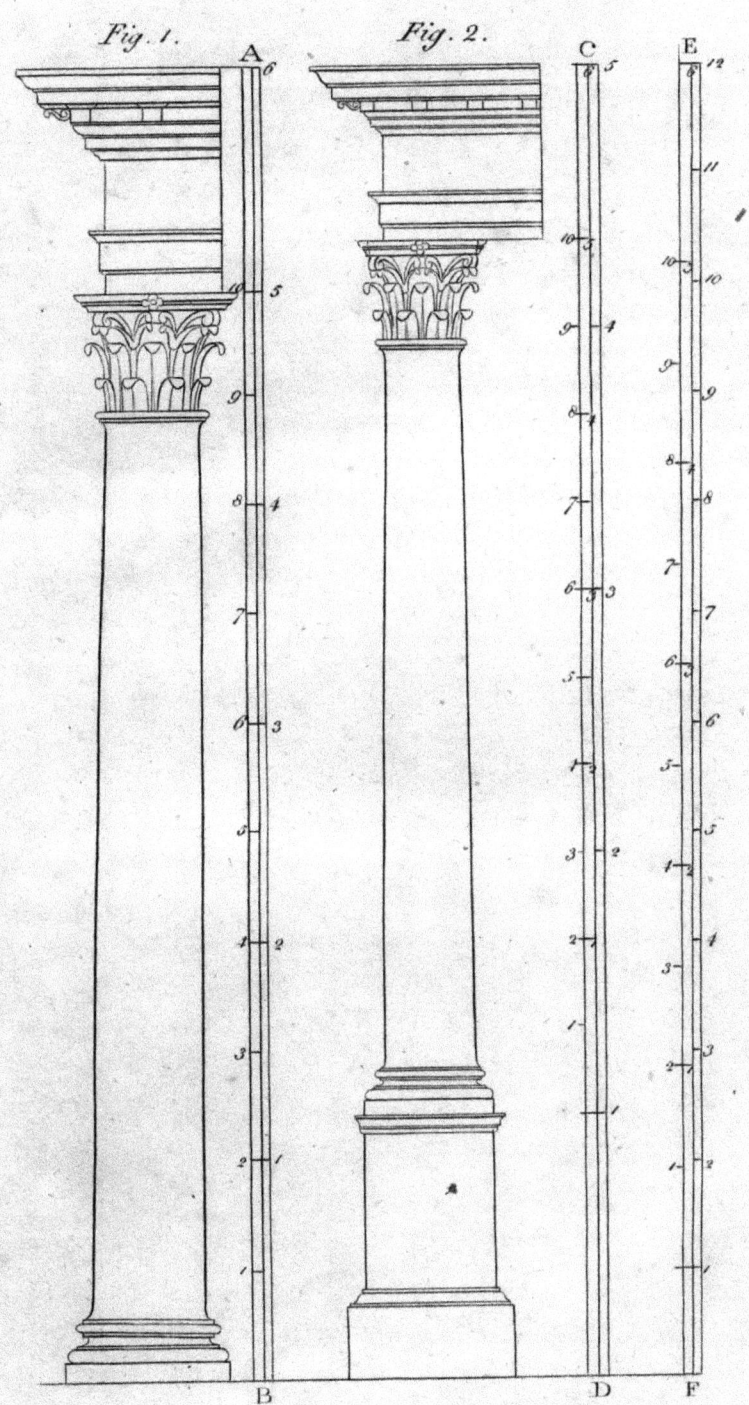

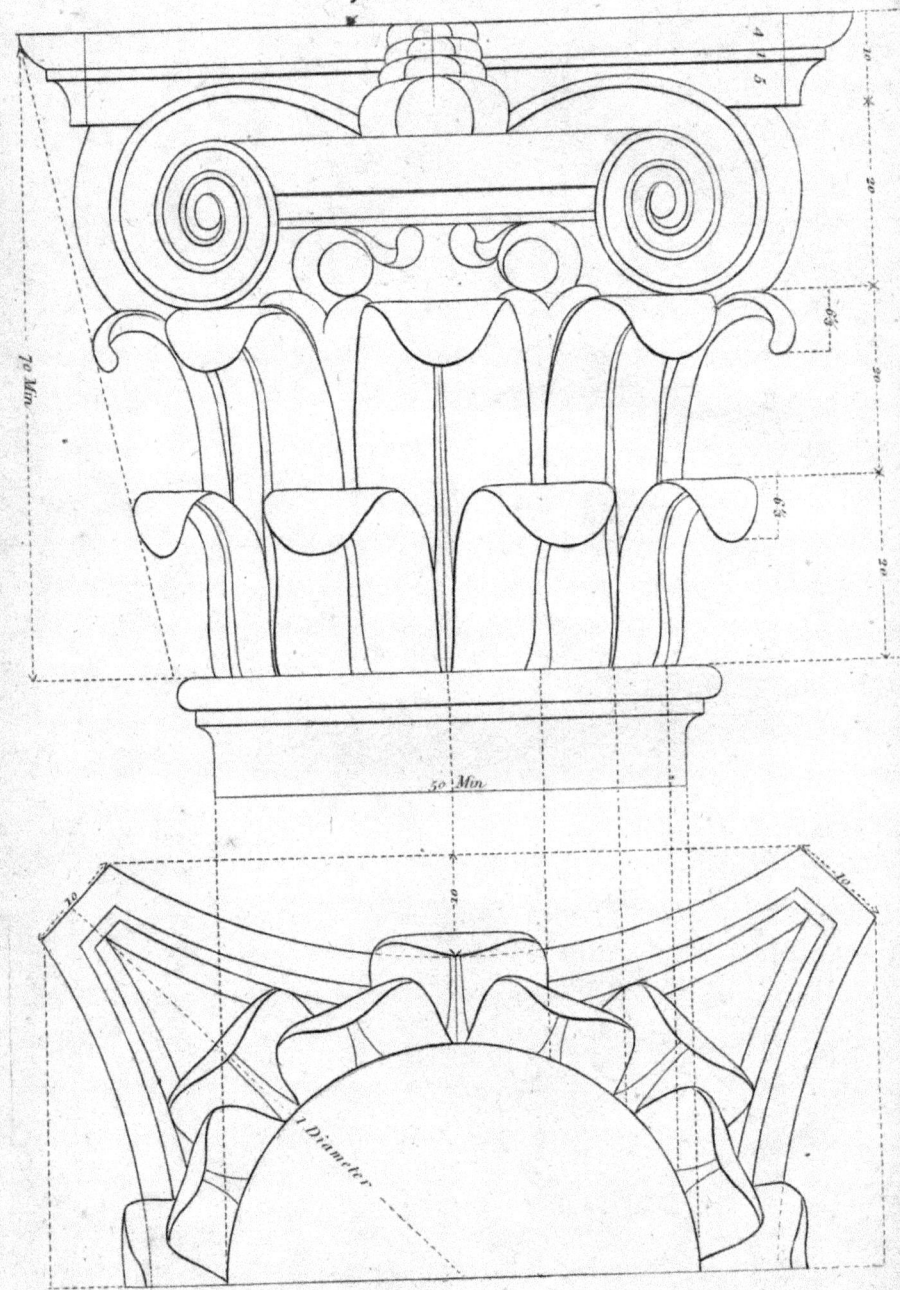

Composite Capital.

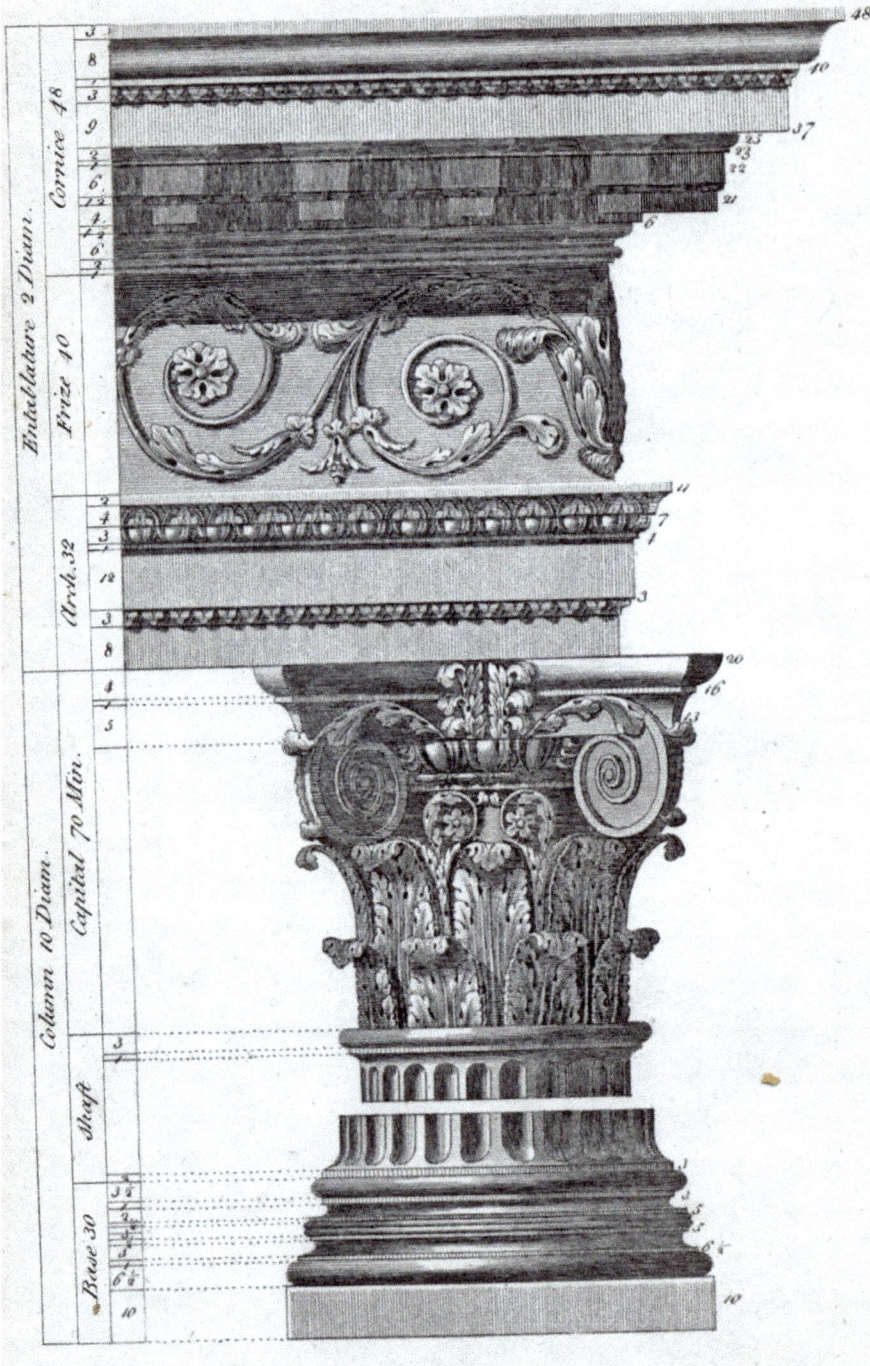

Composite Order.

Pl. 36

OF THE COMPOSITE ORDER.

PLATE XXXV.

General out-line of the Composite capital, shewing the manner of projecting the same.—see the description of Plate 31.

PLATE XXXVI.

Is the Composite order, so named because of its capital; the upper part, being the same as the Ionic angular capital, and the lower part for leaves, the same as the Corinthian; the general heights of the cornice, frize, architrave, capital, shaft, and base, are the same as that of the Corinthian; the diameter of the column is one tenth part of its height, as in the Corinthian; the heights and projections of the members, are plain by the measures on the Plate.

PLATE XXXVII.

Are pedestals for four of the orders. It has been already mentioned, that the pedestal of every order is one fifth of its entire height; the die of the pedestal or plain part, is in breadth, equal to the plinth of the base of the column.

PLATE XXXVIII.

OF BASES.

To each order there is a particular kind of base. A Tuscan base is shewn to Plate 9 and 10. To the Doric there is no particular base, but the Attic base is proper to be used as shewn on Plate 13. The Ionic base is of a clumsy appearance, and is very rarely used, *Fig.* 1. Plate 38. The Corinthian base is very elegant, as is shewn by *Fig.* 2. The Composite base is *Fig.* 3. The Attic base (Plate 13 and 24) is most frequently used, and is applicable to all the orders, except the Tuscan.

METHOD FOR GLUEING UP OF BASES.

Fig. 4. is a plan shewing how the bottom course is mitered together: which must be done on a flat board, and all the joints fitted as close as possible; this course being glued together with care, and well blocked in the inside at the angles, and the glue being thoroughly dry, plane the top of the course quite smooth, and out of winding; then glue on the next course, breaking the joint in the middle of the under course, as shewn by the dotted lines, and so on, for as many courses as wanted: when thoroughly dry it may be sent to the turner. The bedding joints may be on one side of a fillet, as shewn in the elevation, *Fig.* 5. A A, B B, C C: a base glued up in this manner will be the strongest possible, and be less liable to crack and split, than by any other method I have seen practised.

DESIGNS

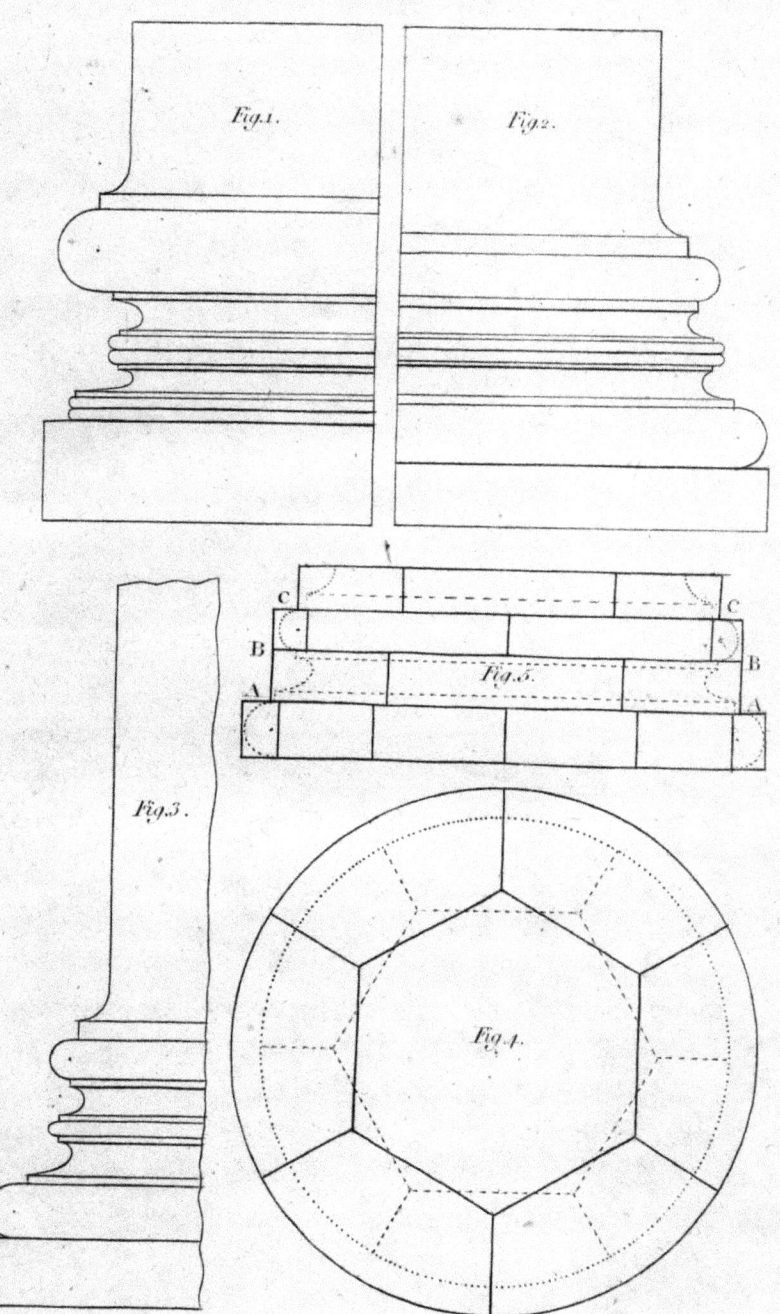

Doric Door.

DESIGNS FOR DOOR CASES.

Plate 39, Is a design for a door case of the Tuscan order.

Plate 40, Is a design for a door case of the Doric order.

Plate 41, Door way and portico from the Ionic Temple on the Illissus, (see Plate 27). That doors of this construction were used by the ancients is evident from the example of the Tower of the Winds, as shewn by Stuart, in *The Antiquities of Athens, vol. I.*

The above are proper examples to draw from, and will give some useful ideas for composition and combinations of the orders, and their parts, and will look well if executed.

FINIS.

A CATALOGUE
OF
MODERN BOOKS
ON
ARCHITECTURE,

Theoretical, Practical, and Ornamental;

VIZ.

BOOKS OF PLANS AND ELEVATIONS
FOR COTTAGES, FARM-HOUSES, MANSIONS, &c.
TEMPLES, BRIDGES, &c.

Of Ornaments for internal Decorations, Foliage for Carvers, &c.

ON PERSPECTIVE.

Books of Use for Carpenters, Bricklayers, and
WORKMEN IN GENERAL, &c. &c.

Which, with the best ANCIENT AUTHORS, are constantly
on SALE at

J. TAYLOR's
ARCHITECTURAL LIBRARY,

No. 59,

HIGH HOLBORN, LONDON.

WHERE MAY BE HAD,
The WORKS of the most celebrated
FRENCH ARCHITECTS and ENGINEERS.

A CATALOGUE, &c.

THE *Antiquities of Athens*; measured and delineated, by *James Stuart*, F. R. S. and F. S. A. and *Nicholas Revett*, Painters and Architects, in four large Volumes Folio, Price 25*l*. 4*s*. in boards.—*This Work contains 384 Plates, engraved by the best Artists, of Views, Architecture, Plans, &c. with Letter-press, Historical and Descriptive, illustrating by a Research of many Years' Labour and great Expense, the purest Examples of Grecian Architecture, many of which no longer exist, and the Traces of them can be found only in this Work.*

Contents of the Work.

Doric Portico at Athens, Ionic Temple on the Ilissus, Octagon Tower of Andronicus Cyrrestes, Lanthorn of Demosthenes, Stoa, or Portico at Athens: And a large View of the Acropolis. Temple of Minerva, Temple of Erectheus, Theatre of Bacchus, Choragic Monument of Thrasyllus, &c. Propylea: And a large View, and a Plan of the Acropolis. Temple of Theseus, Temple of Jupiter, Arch of Theseus, Aqueduct of Hadrian, Monument of Philopappus, Temple of Corinth, Bridge of the Ilissus, Odeum of Regilla, Ruins at Salonica, Antiquities on the Island of Delos, &c.—Also a large Map of Greece—Map of Attica—Plan of Athens, &c.

The Fourth Vol. which is just Published, contains all the remaining Sculpture of the Temple of Minerva at Athens, with sundry Fragments found in the Greek Islands: also the entire Details of the Antiquities at Pola, in Istria, from the Drawings left by *Mr. Stuart.* Engraved on 103 Plates, imperial folio, 7*l*. 7*s*. Boards.

The Third Volume may be had separate, to complete Sets. Price 6*l*. 13*s*. in boards.

An Essay on the Doric Order of Architecture, containing an historical View of its Rise and Progress among the Ancients, with a Critical Investigation of its Principles of Composition and Adaptation to Modern Use, illustrated by Figures from the principal Antique Examples, drawn to one Scale, on 7 Plates, by *E. Aikin*, Architect, large Folio, 1*l*. 5*s*. boards.

The Ancient Buildings of Rome, accurately measured and delineated, by *Antony Desgodetz*, with Explanations in French and English; the Text translated, and the Plates engraved, by the late *Mr. George Marshall*, Architect, 2 vols. imperial folio, with 137 Plates, Price 6*l*. 16*s*. 6*d*. half bound.

Plans, Elevations, Sections and Views of the Church of *Batalha*, in the Province of Estremadura, in Portugal, with an History and Description,

Description, by Father Luis de Sousa, with Remarks, to which is prefixed an Introductory Discourse upon the Principles of Gothic Architecture, by *James Murphy*, Architect. Illustrated with 27 elegant Plates, printed on Imperial Folio, and hot-pressed, Price 4l. 14s. 6d. half-bound.

Specimens of Gothic Architecture, consisting of Doors, Windows, Buttresses, Pinnacles, &c. with the Measurements; selected from Ancient Buildings at Oxford, &c. Drawn and etched by *F. Mackenzie* and *A. Pugin*. On 61 Plates, Quarto, Price 2l. 2s. in Boards, on Demy; and on Imperial Paper, 3l. 3s. Boards; to range with Britton's Architectural Antiquities and Cathedrals.

The Architectural Antiquities of Great Britain, represented and illustrated in a Series of Views, Elevations, Plans, Sections and Details, of Various Ancient English Edifices, with Historical and Descriptive Accounts of each. By *John Britton*, F. S. A. 4 Vols. Quarto, with 278 elegant engraved Plates, 21l. in Boards, and on large Paper 32l.

N. B. The parts may be had separate to complete Sets at 10s. 6d. each, large Paper 16s.

An Historical and Architectural Essay, relating to Redcliffe Church, Bristol, illustrated with 12 engravings of Plans, Views and Details, with an Account of the Monuments, and Anecdotes of eminent Persons connected with the Church. Royal Octavo, 16s. Medium Quarto, 1l. 4s. and Imperial Quarto, 1l. 11s. 6d.

N. B. The Quarto sizes will range with the Architectural Antiques.

The Cathedral Antiquities of England, or an Historical, Architectural and Graphical Illustration of the English Cathedral Churches. By *John Britton*, F. S. A. Of this work, one Part, containing 6 or 7 Plates, is published every three Months, Price 12s. Medium Quarto, and on Imperial Quarto 1l.

N. B. Salisbury Cathedral is completed in 5 Parts.—*Norwich Cathedral* is completed in 4 Parts.—Winchester Cathedral is complete in 5 Parts.—*York* is completed in 6 Parts.—*Litchfield* is now publishing.

The History and Antiquities of the Parochial Church of St. Saviour, Southwark, illustrated by a Series of Engravings of exterior and interior Views, Ground Plan, and Details of that Edifice. From Drawings by *W. G. Moss*. 17 Plates, 4to., Price, in Boards, 1l. 11s. 6d. Proof Impressions on India Paper, 2l. 12s. 6d.

Specimens of Gothic Architecture, selected from the Parish Church of Lavenham, in Suffolk, on 40 Plates quarto. Price 18s. boards, on large Paper, 1l. 5s.

Dickinson's Architectural Antiquities of Southwell, &c. Two Parts, Quarto, with 23 elegant Plates, 1l. 1s. Boards.

Gothic Ornaments of the Cathedral Church of York, by *J. Halfpenny*, 105 Plates, large Quarto.

Fragmenta

Fragmenta Vetusta, or the Ancient Buildings of York, by *J. Halfpenny*, 34 Plates, large Quarto, 3l. 3s.

The Rudiments of Ancient Architecture, containing an Historical Account of the Five Orders, with their Proportions, and Examples of each from Antiques: Also, Extracts from *Vitruvius, Pliny*, &c. relative to the Buildings of the Antients. Calculated for the Use of those who wish to attain a summary Knowledge of the Science of Architecture; with a Dictionary of Terms: illustrated with 11 Plates. The Fourth Edition, Boards, 8s.

Essays on Gothic Architecture, by the Rev. T. Warton, Rev. J. Bentham, Capt. Grose, and Rev. J. Milner. Illustrated with 12 Plates of Ornaments, &c. selected from Ancient Buildings; calculated to exhibit the various Styles of different Periods. The third Edition, with a List of the Cathedrals of England and theirABimensions. Octavo. 10s. 6d. Boards.

An Historical Survey of the Ecclesiastical Antiquities of France, with a View to illustrate the Rise and Progress of Gothic Architecture in Europe. By the late Rev. *G. D. Whittington*, of Cambridge. Elegantly printed in Royal 8vo. With a Frontispiece of the Façade of the Cathedral Church at Rheimes. 12s. Boards.

A Treatise on the *Ecclesiastical Architecture of England*, during the middle Ages, with 10 illustrative Copper Plates, by the Rev. *J. Milner*, D. D. F. S. A. Royal Octavo. 15s. Boards.

Observations on *English Architecture*, Military, Ecclesiastical, and Civil, compared with similar Buildings on the Continent; including a critical Itinerary of *Oxford* and *Cambridge*: also Historical Notices of Stained Glass, Ornamental Gardening, &c. with Chronological Tables, and Dimensions of Cathedrals and Conventual Churches, by the Rev. *James Dallaway*, M. B. F. S. A. Royal Octavo. 12s. Boards.

An Essay on the Origin, History and Principles of Gothic Architecture, by Sir *James Hall*, Bart. large Quarto, handsomely printed, with 60 Plates elegantly engraved, of select Examples, 5l. 5s. in Boards.

The Builder's Price Book; *containing a correct List of the Prices allowed by the most eminent Surveyors in London to the several Artificers concerned in Building: including the Journeymen's Prices.* A new Edition, corrected; by an Experienced Surveyor. Sewed, 3s. 6d.

Vitruvius Britannicus, or the British Architect; containing Plans, Elevations, and Sections of the regular Buildings, both Public and Private, in Great Britain. By *Woolf* and *Gandon*, Architects. 2 Vols. Imperial Folio, 11l. 11s. half bound.

N. B. Gentlemen who wish to bind these Volumes to complete *Campbell's* Vitruvius, may have them in Sheets, Price 10l. 10s.

There are a few Sets on hand of the 3 Volumes by *Campbell*, Price 6l. 6s. in sheets.

The

The *New Vitruvius Britannicus*, consisting of Plans and Elevations of modern Buildings, public and private, erected in Great Britain by the most *celebrated Architects*, engraved on 142 Plates, from original Drawings. By *G. Richardson*, Architect. Two Vols. Imperial Folio, half bound, 11l. 11s.

Sketches for *Cottages, Villas*, &c. with their Plans and appropriate Scenery, by *John Soane*; to which is added six Designs for *improving and embellishing Grounds*, with Explanations, by an *Amateur*, on 54 Plates, elegantly engraved in Aquatinta. Folio. 2l. 12s. 6d. half bound.

Plans, Elevations, and Sections of Buildings, executed in the Counties of *Norfolk, Suffolk, Yorkshire, Wiltshire, Warwickshire, Staffordshire, Somersetshire*, &c. by *John Soane*, Architect, on 47 Folio Plates, 2l. 12s. 6d.

Plans, *Elevations*, and *Sections*, of Noblemen's and Gentlemen's Houses, Stabling, Bridges public and private, Temples, and other Garden Building, executed in the Counties of Derby, Durham, Middlesex, Northumberland, Nottingham, York, Essex, Wilts, Hertford, Suffolk, Salop, and Surrey; by *James Paine*, Architect. Two Vols. with 176 very large Folio Plates, 8l. 8s. half bound.

The Designs of *Inigo Jones*, consisting of Plans and Elevations for Public and Private Buildings; including the Detail of the intended Palace at Whitehall; published by *W. Kent*, with some additional Designs. 2 Vols. Imperial Folio.

Plans, Elevations, and Sections of *Hot-Houses, Green-Houses, an Aquarium, Conservatories*, &c. recently built in different Parts of England for various Noblemen and Gentlemen, by *G. Tod*, Surveyor and Hot-House Builder; including a Hot-House and a Green-House in her Majesty's Gardens at Frogmore, on 27 Plates, elegantly coloured, with proper Descriptions. Folio, 2l. 12s. 6d. in Boards.

Designs for Villas and other Rural Buildings, by *Edmund Aikin*, Architect; with Plans and Explanations. Together with an Introductory Essay, containing Remarks on the prevailing Defects of Modern Architecture, and an Investigation of the Style best adapted to the Dwellings of the present Times; engraved on 31 Plates large Quarto, Price 1l. 11s. 6d. in Boards.

A Series of Designs for Villas and Country Houses. Adapted with Economy to the Comforts and to the Elegancies of Modern Life; with Plans and Explanations to each. To which is prefixed, an Essay on Modern Architectural Taste. By *C. A. Busby*, Architect. Engraved in Aquatinta, on 24 Plates, large Quarto, in Boards, 1l. 5s.

Architectural Designs, for Rustic Cottages, Picturesque Dwellings, Villas, &c. with appropriate Scenery, Plans and Descriptions; to which are prefixed some critical Observations on their Style and Character;

ter; and also of Castles, Abbies, and ancient English Houses.—Concluding with Practical Remarks on Building, and the Causes of the *Dry Rot*. By *W. F. Pocock*, Architect. Elegantly engraved on 33 Plates, Royal Quarto, Price 1l. 11s. 6d. in Boards.

Designs for *Lodges, and Entrances* to Parks, Paddocks, and Pleasure Grounds, in the Gothic, Cottage, and Fancy Styles, with characteristic Scenery and Descriptions in Letter-press, by *T. D. W. Dearn*, elegantly engraved on 20 Plates, large Quarto, 1l. 11s. 6d. Boards.

Sketches in Architecture, consisting of original Designs for Cottages and Rural Dwellings, suitable to Persons of moderate Fortune, and for convenient Retirement; with Plans and appropriate Scenery to each; also some general Observations. By *T. D. W. Dearn*, Architect to his Royal Highness the Duke of Clarence. Elegantly engraved on 20 Plates, large Quarto, Price 1l. 7s. in Boards.

Plans and *Views* of Buildings executed in *England and Scotland* in the Castellated and other Styles. By *R. Lugar, Architect*, on 32 Plates Royal Quarto with descriptive Letter-press, Price 2l. 2s. in boards.

Architectural Sketches for Cottages, Rural Dwellings, and Villas: with Plans, suitable to Persons of genteel Life and moderate Fortune: proper for Picturesque Buildings, by *R. Lugar*, Architect and Land Surveyor; elegantly engraved in Aquatinta, on 38 Plates, Boards, 1l. 11s. 6d.

The Country Gentleman's Architect, containing a Variety of Designs for Farm Houses and Farm Yards of Different Magnitudes, arranged on the most approved Principles for Arable, Grazing, Feeding and Dairy Farms, with Plans and Sections, shewing at large the Construction of Cottages, Barns, Stables, Feeding Houses, Dairies, Brewhouse, &c. with Plans for Stables and Dog-kennels, and some Designs for Labourers' Cottages and small Villas. The whole adapted to the Use of Country Gentlemen about to build or to alter. Engraved on 21 Plates, with some General Observations, and full Explanations to each. By *R. Lugar.* Quarto, 1l. 5s. in Boards.

Designs for *Small Picturesque Cottages, Hunting Boxes, Park Entrances*, &c. by *E. Gyfford*, Architect. Part I. Engraved in Aquatinta, on 20 Plates, Quarto, 1l. 1s. Boards.

Designs for *Elegant Cottages*, and small Villas, calculated for the Comfort and Convenience of Persons of moderate and of ample Fortune, carefully studied and thrown into Perspective, with General Estimates, by *E. Gyfford*, Architect. Part II. Engraved in Aquatinta on 26 Plates, Quarto 1l. 11s. 6d. boards.

Hints for Dwellings, consisting of Original Designs for Cottages, Farm-houses, Villas, &c. plain and ornamental; with Plans to each, in which strict Attention is paid to unite Convenience and Elegance with Economy. Including some Designs for Town-houses. By *D. Laing*, Architect, and Surveyor. Elegantly engraved

graved on 34 Plates in Aquatinta, with appropriate Scenery. Quarto, 1l. 5s. in boards.

Sketches for Country Houses, Villas, and Rural Dwellings; calculated for Persons of moderate Income, and for comfortable Retirement. Also some Designs for Cottages, which may be constructed of the simplest Materials; with Plans and general Estimates. By *John Plaw*. Elegantly engraved in Aquatinta on 42 Plates, Quarto, 1l. 11s. 6d. in Boards.

Ferme Ornée, or *Rural Improvements*, a Series of Domestic and Ornamental Designs; suited to Parks, Plantations, Rides, Walks, Rivers, Farms, &c. consisting of Fences, Paddock House, a Bath, Dog-kennels, Pavilions, Farm-yards, Fishing-houses, Sporting-Boxes, Shooting-lodges, Single and Double Cottages, &c. calculated for Landscape and Picturesque Effects. By *John Plaw*, Architect. Engraved in Aquatinta on 38 Plates, with appropriate Scenery. Plans, and Explanations. Quarto. In Boards, 1l. 11s. 6d.

An Essay on British Cottage Architecture, exemplified by fourteen Designs, with their Plans, &c. on 23 Plates, designed and executed by *James Malton*. The Second Edition, with two additional Plates, large Quarto, Boards, 1l. 11s. 6d.

A Collection of *Architectural Designs*, for Villas, Casinos, Mansions, Lodges, and Cottages, from original Drawings, by *James Randall*, Architect, engraved in Aquatinta, on 34 Plates, Folio, 2l. 12s. 6d.

The Architect and Builder's Miscellany, or Pocket Library; containing original Picturesque Designs in Architecture, for Cottages, Farm, Country, and Town Houses, Public Buildings, Temples, Greenhouses, Bridges, Lodges and Gates for Entrances to Parks and Pleasure Grounds, Stables, Monumental Tombs, Garden Seats, &c. By *Charles Middleton*, Architect. On 60 Plates, coloured. Octavo. 1l. 1s. bound.

Crunden's Convenient and Ornamental Architecture; consisting of Original Designs for Plans, Elevations and Sections, beginning with the Farm-house, and regularly ascending to the most grand and magnificent Villa; calculated both for Town and Country, with Explanation in Letter-press, and exact Scales. Engraved on 70 Copper-plates, 16s. Boards.

A Series of Plans, for Cottages or Habitations for the Labourer, either in Husbandry or the Mechanic Arts, adapted as well to Towns as to the Country. To which is added, an Introduction, containing many useful Observations on this Class of building, tending to the Comfort of the Poor, and Advantage of the Builder; with Calculations of Expenses. By the late *Mr. J. Wood*, of Bath, Architect. A new Edition, corrected to the present Time, with 30 Plates, large 4to. 1l. 1s.

The Country Gentleman's Architect, in a great Variety of New Designs for Cottages, Farm-houses, Country-houses, Villas, Lodges for Park

Park or Garden Entrances, and ornamental wooden Gates, with Plans of the Offices belonging to each Design; distributed with a strict Attention to Convenience, Elegance and Economy. On 32 Quarto Plates. By *J. Miller*, Architect. Sewed, 10s. 6d.

Essays of the London Architectural Society. Octavo, 4 Plates. 7s. Boards. Also the Second Part, 4 Plates, 8s. 6d.

Aikin's Essay on the Doric Order, 7 Plates, Imperial Folio. 1l. 5s. Boards.

Vitruvius Britannicus, by *Campbell*, 3 Vols. Folio, 6l. 6s. in Sheets.

The Continuation to Campbell, by *Woolf* and *Gandon*, Vol. 4 and 5, 10l. 10s. in Sheets.

Chambers's (Sir William) Treatise on Civil Architecture.

Chambers's Buildings and Views of Kew Gardens. Half bound, 2l. 10s.

Chambers's Designs for Chinese Buildings, &c. 1l. 11s. 6d.

Chambers's Dissertation on Oriental Gardening, 4to. 9s.

Gwilt on Arches, 8vo. 4 Plates. 6s.

Ware on Arches, and their abutment Piers, octavo, 19 Plates. 18s.

Ware's Remarks on Theatres, octavo, 3 Plates. 7s.

Atwood on Arches, quarto, Two Parts. Plates. 18s.

Malton (James) Perspective, Quarto, 1l. 1s.

Paine's Plans, Elevations, &c. of Noblemen's Seats, &c. folio, 2 vols. Half bound, 8l. 8s.

The Architectural Antiquities of Athens, by Stuart, 4 vols. of Rome, Balbec, Palmyra, Pœstum, Ionia, de la Grece, par *Le Roy*, &c. &c.

The Unedited Antiquities of Attica, by the Society of Dilettanti, Folio, elegantly engraved and printed, 10l. 10s. boards.

Pompeiana, by *Gell* and *Gandy*. Octavo. 5l. 15s. 6d.

Delineations of Pompeii, by *Major Cockburn*. Folio.

Allason's Views of the Antiquities of Pola. Folio.

Wilkins' Antiquities of Magna Græcia, &c. Folio.

Wilkins' Translation of Vitruvius, 2 vols. Quarto, 6l. 6s.

Newton's Translation of Vitruvius, 2 vols. folio.

Murphy's Arabian Antiquities of Spain, 100 Plates, large folio, 42l.

Nicholson's Principles of Architecture, 3 vols. 8vo. 3l. 3s. boards.

Nicholson's Architectural Dictionary, 2 Vols. 4to.

Tatham's Etchings of Ancient Ornamental Architecture. 100 Plates. Folio. 4l. 4s. boards.

A Treatise on Theatres, including some Experiments on Sound, by G. *Saunders*, Architect, with Plates, 4to. boards, 16s.

Smeaton's

Smeaton's Description of the Edystone Lighthouse, Plates, folio. 6l. 6s.
Reports, by *J. Smeaton*, Civil Engineer, 3 vols. 4to. 7l. 7s. Boards.
Smeaton's Miscellaneous Papers, 4to. 1l. 11s. 6d. Boards.
Gray's Experienced Millwright. Folio, 44 Plates. 2l. 2s.
Banks on Mills, octavo, Plates. 10s. 6d. boards.
Buchanan's Practical Essays on Mill-Work. 2 Vol. 19s. boards.
Gregory's Treatise on Mechanics, 3 Vols. 2l. 2s.
Hutton's Course of Mathematics. 3 Vols. 1l. 11s. 6d.
Hutton's Tracts on Mathematical and Philosophical Subjects, &c. 3 Vols. 2l. 2s.
Papworth on the Dry Rot, 3s.
Randall on the Dry Rot, 3s.
M'William on the Dry Rot and Forest Trees, quarto, 1l. 11s. 6d.
Perronet sur les Ponts, 2 Tom.
Belidor Science des Ingeneurs, 4to. New Edition, with new Plates, &c.
Belidor, l'Architecture Hydraulique, 4 Tom. Quarto.
Nouvelle Arch. Hydraulique, par Prony, 2 Tom.
Piranesi's Works, complete, 23 Vols. large Folio.
Rafael's Ornaments of the Vatican, 3 Parts, Folio.
Dictionnaire d'Architecture, Civile, Militaire et Navale, par Roland, 3 Tom. Quarto, with 100 Plates.
Plans, Coupes, et Elevations des plus belles Maisons et des Hotels, à Paris, et dans les Environs, avec des Ornemens. Folio, 120 Plates.
Durand Leçons d'Architecture, 2 Tom. 4to.
Durand Recueil et Parallele des Edifices Anciens et Modernes. 92 very large folio Plates.
Plans, Coupes et Elevations de diverses Productions de l'Art de la Charpente, par Krafft. 201 Plates, large Folio.
Ornamenti di Albertoli, 3 Parts, Folio.
Museo Pio Clementino, 7 Tom.
Museo Chiaramonti.
Wiebeking on Bridges, Draining, &c. In German. 4 Vols. 4to. and a large Atlas.
Wiebeking des Ponts à Arches de Charpente, 4to. with a large Atlas of 20 plates.
Ornemens de le Pautre. 3 Vols. Folio.
Bourse de Paris, par Brouginard.
Œuvres de Weyrotter.

Voyage

Voyage de la Grece, par Choiseuil Gouffiere. 2 Vols.
Antiquité de Poestum, par Delagardette. Folio.
Ornemens de Cauvet. Folio.
Voyage Pittoresque de l'Istria, par Casas. Folio.
Voyage Pittoresque de la Suisse. 4 Vols. Folio.
Voyage Pittoresque de Naple et Sicile. 5 Vols. Folio.
Voyage Pittoresque des Isles de Sicile, de Malte et de Lipari, par Houel. 4 Vols. Folio.
Suite de Paysage, de Bourgin. Folio.
Cabinet de Poulain. Proofs.
Coupe de Pierre, par Gardelle.
Canaux Navigables, de Lalande, Folio.
Canal du Midi, par Andreossi. 2 Vols. 4to.
Encyclopedie de l'Ingenieur, par Delaitre. 3 Vols. 8vo. and Atlas of Plates.
Pousse des Terres, par Maignes, 4to.
Traité de l'Art de Batir, par Rondelet. 5 Vols 4to. Plates.
Programme du Course de Construction, par Sganzin, 4to.
Decorations par Percier et Fontains, Folio.
Palais et Maisons de Rome, par Percier, Folio.
Italia avant il Dominio di Romani, par Micali. 4 Vols. 8vo. and Atlas.
Manuel du Tourneur. 2 Vols. 4to. Plates.
Dictionnaire des Graveurs. 2 Vols. 8vo. Plates.
Memoire de l'Architecture, par Patte, 4to.
Coupe de Pierres, de Freziere, 3 Vols. 4to.
Description du Pont à Moulins, par Régemorte, Folio.
Boulet Machines de Theatre.
Scrittori dell'acqua. 8 Vols. 4to.
Paris et ses Monumens, par Baltard. Folio.
Musée des Monumens Francais, par Lenoir. 6 Vol. 8vo.
Annales du Musée, par Landon.
Bossut Traité d'Hydrodynamique. 2 Vols. 8vo.
Bossut et Viallet sur la Construction des Digues.
Bremontier sur le Mouvement des Ondes.
Decessart Travaux Hydrauliques. 2 Vols. 4to.
Ducrest D'Hydrauferie.
Les Fontaines de Paris, par Duval.
Gauthey de la Construction des Ponts. 3 Vols. 4to.

Lesage

Lesage divers Memoires des Ponts et Chaussées. 2 Vols. 4to.

Navier, Projet d'une Gare à Choisy.

Sakolniki Hydrodynamique.

Berard Statique des Voûtes.

Brunet, dimension des Fers qui doivent former la coupole de la Halle aux Grains.

Pyre, Restauration du Pantheon.

Clochar Plans de Maisons, &c. D'Italie. Folio.

Costume Hollandoise. Plates, coloured.

Voyage en Holland. 3 Vols. 8vo. Plates.

Statistique d'Amsterdam.

Guide du Voyageur en Hollande.

New Principles of Linear Perspective, or the Art of Designing on a Plane, the representation of all Sorts of Objects in a more general and simple Method than has been hitherto done. Illustrated by 13 Quarto Plates. By *Dr. Brook Taylor,* LL.D. and R.SS. The Fourth Edition, 8vo. 14s. in boards.

Dr. Brook Taylor's Method of Perspective made easy both in Theory and Practice; in two Books: being an Attempt to make the Art of Perspective easy and familiar, to adapt it entirely to the Arts of Design, and to make it an entertaining Study to any Gentleman who shall choose so Polite an Amusement. By *Joshua Kirby.* Illustrated with 35 Copper-plates. The Third Edition, with several Additions and Improvements. Elegantly printed on Imperial Paper. Half Bound, 2l. 12s. 6d.

The Perspective of Architecture, a Work entirely new; deduced from the Principles of Dr. Brook Taylor, and performed by two Rules of universal Application. Illustrated with 73 Plates. Begun by Command of his present Majesty when Prince of Wales. By *Joshua Kirby.* Elegantly printed on Imperial Paper. 3l. 3s. half bound.

The Description and Use of a new Instrument called the Architectonic Sector, by which any Part of Architecture may be drawn with Facility and Exactness. By *Joshua Kirby.* Illustrated with 25 Plates; elegantly printed on imperial Paper. Half bound, 1l. 16s.

The two Frontispieces, by Hogarth, to Kirby's Perspective, may be had separate, each 5s.

Modern Finishings for Rooms, a Series of Designs for Vestibules, Halls, Stair Cases, Dressing Rooms, Boudoirs, Libraries, and Drawing Rooms, with their Doors, Chimney Pieces, and other finishings to a large Scale, and the several Mouldings and Cornices at full Size, showing their Construction and relative Proportions: to which are added some Designs for Villas and Porticos, with the Rules for drawing the Columns, &c. at large. The whole adapted for the
Use

Use and Direction of every Person engaged in the practical Parts of Building, by *W. F. Pocock*, Architect, on 86 Plates, quarto, 2l. 2s. bound.

The Student's Instructor in drawing and working the Five Orders of Architecture; fully explaining the best Methods of striking regular and quirked Mouldings, for diminishing and glueing of Columns and Capitals, for finding the true Diameter of an Order to any given Height, for striking the Ionic Volute circular and elliptical, with finished Examples, on a large Scale, of the Orders, their Planceers, &c. and some Designs for Door Cases, by *Peter Nicholson*, engraved on 41 Plates octavo. 10s. 6d. bound. A new Edition corrected and much enlarged.

The Carpenter's New Guide, being a complete Book of Lines for Carpentry and Joinery, treating fully on Practical Geometry, Soffits, Brick and Plaster Groins, Niches of every Description, Sky-lights, Lines for Roofs and Domes, with a great Variety of Designs for Roofs, Trussed Girders, Floors, Domes, Bridges, &c. Stair-cases and Hand-rails of various Constructions. Angle-Bars for Shop Fronts, and Raking Mouldings, with many other Things entirely new: the Whole founded on true Geometrical Principles, the Theory and Practice well explained and fully exemplified on 84 Copper-Plates; including some Observations and Calculations on the Strength of Timber, by *P. Nicholson*, 4to. 1l. 1s. the Sixth Edition corrected and enlarged.

The Carpenter and Joiner's Assistant, containing Practical Rules for making all Kinds of Joints, and various Methods of Hingeing them together; for hanging of Doors on straight or circular Plans; for fitting up Windows and Shutters to answer various Purposes, with Rules for hanging them; for the Construction of Floors, Partitions, Soffits, Groins, Arches for Masonry: for constructing Roofs in the best Manner from a given Quantity of Timber; for placing of Bond-Timbers; with various Methods for adjusting Raking Pediments, enlarging and diminishing of Mouldings, taking Dimensions for Joinery, and for setting out Shop Fronts; with a new Scheme for constructing Stairs and Hand-rails, and for stairs having a conical Well-hole, &c. &c. To which are added, Examples of Various Roofs executed, with the Scantlings from actual Measurements, with Rules for Mortices and Tenons, and for fixing Iron Straps, &c. Also Extracts from M. Belidor, M. du Hamel, M. de Buffon, &c. on the Strength of Timber, with practical Observations. Illustrated with 79 Plates, and copious Explanations. By *Peter Nicholson*. Quarto 1l. 1s. bound. The fourth Edition, revised and corrected.

The Practical House Carpenter, or Youth's Instructor: containing a great Variety of useful Designs in Carpentry and Architecture; as Centering for Groins, Niches, &c. Examples for Roofs, Sky-lights, &c. The Five Orders laid down by a New Scale. Mouldings, &c. at large, with their Enrichments. Plans, Elevations, and Sections

of

of Houses for Town and Country, Lodges, Hot-houses, Greenhouses, Stables, &c. Design for a Church, with Plan, Elevation, and two Sections; an Altar-piece, and Pulpit. Designs for Chimney-pieces, Shop Fronts, Door Cases. Section of a Dining-room and Library. Variety of Stair Cases, with many other important Articles and useful Embellishments. To which is added, a List of Prices for Materials and Labour, Labour only, and Day Prices. The whole illustrated and made perfectly easy by 148 quarto Copper-plates, with Explanations to each. By *William Pain*. The sixth Edition, with large Additions. 18s. bound.

N. B. This is PAIN's last Work.

The Carpenter's Pocket Directory: containing the best Methods of framing Timbers of all Figures and Dimensions, with their several Parts; as Floors, Roofs in Ledgements, their Length and Backings; Trussed Roofs, Spires, and Domes, Trussing Girders, Partitions, and Bridges, with Abutments; Centering for Arches, Vaults, &c. cutting Stone Ceilings, Groins, &c. with their Moulds: Centres for drawing Gothic Arches, Ellipses, &c. With the Plan and Sections of a Barn. Engraved on 24 Plates, with Explanations. By *W. Pain*, Architect and Carpenter. Bound, 5s.

Decorations for Parks and Gardens; Designs for Gates, Garden Seats, Alcoves, Temples, Baths, Entrance Gates, Lodges, Facades, Prospect Towers, Cattle Sheds, Ruins, Bridges, Green-houses, &c. &c. Also a Hot-house, and Hot-wall, with Plans and Scales; neatly engraved on 55 Plates, octavo. 10s. 6d. sewed.

Designs in Architecture, consisting of Plans, Elevations, and Sections for Temples, Baths, Cassinos, Pavilions, Garden Seats, Obelisks, and other Buildings; for decorating Pleasure-grounds, Parks, Forests, &c. &c. by *John Soane.* Engraved on 38 Copper-plates, 8vo. Sewed, 6s.

Grotesque Architecture, or Rural Amusement; consisting of Plans, and Elevations, for Huts, Hermitages, Chinese, Gothic and Natural Grottos, Moresque Pavilions, &c. many of which may be executed with Flints, irregular Stones, rude Branches and Roots of Trees; containing 28 Designs. By *W. Wright.* Octavo. Sewed, 4s. 6d.

Ideas for Rustic Furniture, proper for Garden Chairs, Summer Houses, Hermitages, Cottages, &c. engraved on 25 Plates. Octavo. Price 4s.

Designs for Gates and Rails, suitable to Parks, Pleasure-Grounds, Balconies, &c. Also some Designs for Trellis Work. On 27 Plates. By *C. Middleton.* Octavo, 6s.

The Carpenter's Treasure: a Collection of Designs for Temples, with their Plans; Gates, Doors, Rails, and Bridges, in the Gothic Taste, with Centres at large for striking Gothic Curves and Mouldings, and some Specimens of Rails in the Chinese Taste, forming a complete System for Rural Decorations. By *N. Wallis,* Architect. 16 Plates. Octavo. Sewed, 2s. 6d.

Gothic

Gothic Architecture improved, by Rules and Proportions in many grand Designs of Columns, Doors, Windows, Chimney-Pieces, Arcades, Colonnades, Porticos, Umbrellas, Temples, Pavilions, &c. with Plans, Elevations, and Profiles, geometrically exemplified. By B. & T. *Langley*. To which is added, an Historical Discourse on Gothic Architecture. On 64 Plates Quarto. Bound, 15s.

Designs for *Monuments*, including *Grave-stones, Compartments, Wall-pieces*, and *Tombs*. Elegantly engraved on 40 quarto Plates. Half bound, 16s.

Designs for *Shop Fronts* and *Door Cases*, on 27 Plates. 4to. 10s. 6d.

Outlines of Designs for *Shop Fronts* and *Door Cases*, with the Mouldings at large, and Enrichments to each Design. Engraved on 24 Plates. Quarto, 5s.

Langley's Builder's Jewel. Bound, 5s.

Hawney's Complete Measurer, a new Edition, much improved, 4s. 6d.

Hoppus's Timber Measurer. Tables ready cast. 4s.

Plate Glass Book. 4s.

Tariff of Prices of the British Plate Glass Manufactory, 3s. 6d.

The Joiner and Cabinet-maker's Darling; containing sixty different Designs for all Sorts of Frets, Friezes, &c. Sewed, 3s.

The Carpenter's Companion; containing 33 Designs for all Sorts of Chinese Railing and Gates. Octavo. Sewed, 2s.

The Carpenter's Complete Guide to the whole System of Gothic Railing; containing 32 Designs, with Scales to each. Octavo. Sewed, 2s.

A Geometrical View of the Five Orders of Columns in Architecture adjusted by aliquot Parts; whereby the meanest Capacity, by Inspection, may delineate and work an entire Order, or any Part, of any Magnitude required. On a large Sheet, 1s.

Elevation of the New Bridge at Black Friars, with the Plan of the Foundation and Superstructure. by R. *Baldwin*; 12 Inches by 48 Inches, 5s.

Plans, Elevations, and Sections of the Machines and Centering used in erecting Black Friars' Bridge; drawn and engraved by R. *Baldwin*, Clerk of the Work; on 7 large Plates, with Explanations. 10s. 6d.

Elevation of the *Stone Bridge* built over the Severn at *Shrewsbury*; with the Plan of the Foundation and Superstructure, elegantly engraved by *Rooker*. 1s. 6d.

A Treatise on Building in Water. By G. *Semple*. Quarto, with 63 Plates.

Plans, Elevation and Sections of the curious Wooden Bridge at *Schaffhausen* in Switzerland, built in 1760 by *Ulric Grubenman*, and lately destroyed by the French. 19 Inches by 29. Price 12s. coloured, with a descriptive Account in Letter-Press.

Perspective

Perspective View of the proposed Iron Bridge at London, of 600 Feet Span; by *Telford.* Size 4 Feet by 2 Feet, Coloured 2l. 2s.

Observations on *Brick Bond,* as practised at various periods; containing an Investigation of the best Disposition of Bricks in a Wall, for procuring the greatest possible Strength; with Figures representing the different Modes of Construction. Octavo, 1s.

The Bricklayer's Guide to the Mensuration of all Sorts of Brick Work, according to the *London Practice:* With Observations on the Causes and Cure of Smoky Chimnies, the Formation of Drains, and the best Construction of Ovens, to be heated with Coals. Also, a Variety of Practical and Useful Information on this important Branch of the Building Art. Illustrated by various Figures and Nine Copper Plates. By *T. W. Dearn,* Architect. Octavo, 7s. Boards.

Tables for the Purchasing of Estates, Freehold, Copyhold, or Leasehold, Annuities, &c. and for the renewing of Leases held under Cathedral Churches, Colleges, or other Corporate Bodies, for Terms or Years certain, and for Lives. Together with several useful and interesting Tables, connected with the subject. Also the Five Tables of compound Interest. By *W. Inwood,* Architect and Surveyor. In small Octavo for a Pocket Book, 7s. in Boards. Second Edition, enlarged.

BOOKS OF ORNAMENTS, &c.

A Collection of Antique Vases, Altars, Pateras, Tripods, Candelabra, Sarcophagi, &c. from various Museums and Collections, engraved in Outline on 170 Plates, by *H. Moses,* with Historical Essays. 3l. 3s. Half Bound small Quarto, and on large fine Paper, 5l. 5s. in extra Boards.

Select Greek and Roman Antiquities, from Vases, Gems, and other Subjects of the choicest Workmanship. Engraved on 36 Plates, by H. Moses, with Descriptions. Quarto 1l. 1s. boards.

Ornamental Designs after the Manner of the Antique. Composed for the Use of Architects, Ornamental Painters, Statuaries, Carvers, Carpet, Silk, and printed Calico Manufacturers, and every Trade dependent on the Fine Arts, by *G. Smith,* with Descriptions. Quarto. Neatly engraved in Outline. Royal 4to. on 43 Plates, Price 2l. 2s. in Boards.

A Collection of Designs for Modern Embellishments suitable to Parlours, Dining and Drawing Rooms, Folding Doors, Chimney Pieces, Varandas, Frizes, &c. By *C. A. Busby, Architect*; neatly engraved on 24 Plates, 14 of which are elegantly coloured; large Quarto. Price 1l. 11s. 6d.

Designs for the Decoration of Rooms in the various Styles of modern Embellishment. With Pilasters and Frizes at large. On 20 folio Plates, Drawn and Etched by *G. Cooper,* Draftsman and Decorator. 1l. 1s.

Ornaments

Ornaments Displayed, on a full Size for working, proper for all Carvers, Painters, &c. containing a Variety of accurate Examples of Foliage and Frizes, elegantly engraved in the Manner of Chalks, on 33 large Folio Plates. Sewed, 15s.

Pergolesi's Ornaments in the Etruscan and Grotesque Styles, large Folio, Boards.

A New Book of Ornaments; containing a Variety of elegant Designs for modern Pannels, commonly executed in Stucco, Wood, or Painting, and used in Decorating principal Rooms. Drawn and etched by *P. Columbani.* Quarto. Sewed, 7s. 6d.

The Principles of Drawing Ornaments made easy, by proper Examples of Leaves for Mouldings, Capitals, Scrolls, Husks, Foliage, &c. Engraved in Imitation of Drawings, on 16 Plates, with Instructions for learning without a Master. Particularly useful to Carvers, Cabinet-makers, Stucco-workers, Painters, Smiths, and every one concerned in Ornamental Decorations. By *an Artist.* Quarto. Sewed, 4s. 6d.

Ornamental Iron Work, or Designs in the present Taste, for Fanlights, Stair-Case Railing, Window Guard Irons, Lamp-Irons, Palisadoes, and Gates. With a Scheme for adjusting Designs with Facility and Accuracy to any Slope. Engraved on 21 Plates. Quarto. Sewed, 6s.

A new Book of Ornaments, by S. Alken, on 6 Plates, sewed, 2s. 6d.

Law's new Book of Ornaments. Sewed, 2s.

A Collection of Vases from the Antique, &c. on 42 Quarto Plates, Price 7s. Sewed.

An interior View of *Durham Cathedral,* and a View of the elegant *Gothic Shrine* in the same. Elegantly engraved on two large Sheets. Size 19 by 22. The Pair 12s.

An exterior and interior View of *St. Giles's Church in the Fields,* engraved by Walker. Size 18 Inches by 15. The Pair 5s.

A North-west View of Greenwich Church, 2s.

A View of the Roman Catholic Chapel at *Glasgow.* By *Gillespie* and *Lazars.* 1l. 1s. Proofs, 2l. 2s.

A View of Shoreditch Church, 38 Inches by 20, 3s.

An elegant engraved View of the *Monument* at *London,* with the Parts geometrically; Size 21 by 33 Inches, from an Original, by Sir C. Wren, 7s. 6d.

Sir Christopher Wren's Plan for rebuilding the *City* of *London* after the great Fire, 1666. 1s.

West Elevation of *York Minster,* elegantly engraved from a Drawing by *James Malton,* Price 15s.

The Building Act of the 14th Geo. III. with Plates shewing the proper Thickness of Party Walls, External Walls, and Chimneys. A Complete

complete Index, List of Surveyors and their Residences, &c. In a small Pocket Size. Sewed, 3s.

N. B. The Notice and Certificate required by the above Act, may be had printed with blank Spaces for filling up, Price 2d. each, or 13 for 2s.

Experiments and Observations made with a View of improving the Art of composing and applying *Calcareous Cements*, and of preparing *Quick Lime*; with the Theory of these Arts. By *B. Higgins*, M. D.

A General History of Inland Navigation, Foreign and Domestic; containing a Complete Account of the Canals already executed in England; with Considerations on those projected: to which are added, Practical Observations. A new Edit. Octavo, 10s. 6d. Boards.

A Map of England, shewing the Lines of the Canals executed, those proposed, and the navigable Rivers, coloured. On a large Sheet, 5s.

A Treatise on the Improvement of Canal Navigation, exhibiting the numerous Advantages to be derived from *Small Canals* and Boats of two to five Feet wide, containing from two to five Tons Burthen; with a Description of the Machinery for facilitating Conveyance by Water, through the most mountainous Countries, independent of Locks and Aqueducts; including Observations on the great Importance of Water Communications; with Thoughts on, and Designs for, Aqueducts and Bridges of Iron and Wood. By *R. Fulton*, Engineer. With 17 Plates. Quarto, Boards, 18s.

Observations on the various Systems of Canal Navigation, with Inferences practical and mathematical, in which Mr. Fulton's Plan of Wheel Boats, and the Utility of subterraneous and small Canals are particularly investigated; including an Account of the Canals and inclined Planes of China, with 4 Plates. By *W. Chapman*, Civil Engineer. Quarto. 6s. sewed.

Remarkable Ruins and Romantic Prospects of North Britain, with ancient Monuments and singular Subjects of Natural History, by the *Rev. C. Cordiner*, of Banff, with 100 Plates, elegantly engraved by Mazell. 2 Vols. Quarto. 5l. 5s. Boards.

A new Collection of 100 Views in Rome and its Vicinity, neatly engraved by *Pronti*, Quarto, Price 1l. 1s.

A Treatise on Painting, by *Leonardo da Vinci*. Faithfully translated from the original Italian, and now first digested under proper Heads, By *J. F. Rigaud*, *Esq*. R. A. Illustrated with 23 Copper Plates and other Figures. To which is prefixed, a new Life of the Author, drawn up from authentic Materials till now inaccessible, by *J. S. Hawkins*, *Esq*. F. A. S. Royal Octavo, 13s. 6d. Boards.

An Enquiry into the Changes of Taste in Landscape Gardening; to which are added, some Observations on its Theory and Practice, including a Defence of the Art. By *H. Repton*, Esq. Octavo, 5s.

Lectures on the Art of Engraving, delivered at the Royal Institution of Great Britain. By *John Landseer*, Engraver to the King. Octavo, Price 10s. 6d. Boards.

Specimens of Ancient Carpentry, consisting of Framed Roofs selected from various Ancient Buildings, Public and Private. Also some Specimens of Mouldings for Cornices, Doors, and Windows, by the late Mr. *James Smith*, engraved on 36 Plates, Quarto, Price 12s. sewed.

A COLLECTION of DESIGNS for Household Furniture and interior Decoration, in the most approved and elegant Taste, viz. Curtains, Draperies, Beds, Cornices, Chairs and Sofas for Parlors, Libraries, Drawing Rooms, &c. Library Fauteuils, Seats, Ottomans, Chaise Longue, Tables for Libraries, Writing, Work, Dressing, &c. Sideboards, Celerets, Book-cases, Screens, Candelabri, Chiffoniers, Commodes, Pier Tables, Wardrobes, Pedestals, Glasses, Mirrors, Lamps, Jardiniers, &c. with various Designs for Rooms, Geometrical and in Perspective, shewing the Decorations, Adjustment of the Furniture, and also some general Observations, and a Description of each Plate. By GEORGE SMITH, Upholder Extraordinary to his Royal Highness the Prince of Wales. Elegantly engraved on 158 Plates, with Descriptions. Royal Quarto, Price 4l. 14s. 6d. in Boards, and elegantly coloured 7l. 17s. 6d.

Designs for *Household Furniture*, exhibiting a Variety of Elegant and Useful Patterns, in the Cabinet, Chair, and Upholstery Branches. By the late *T. Sheraton*. Engraved on 84 Folio Plates, Price 3l. 13s. 6d. in Boards.

Mechanical Exercises; or, the Elements and Practice of Carpentry, Joinery, Bricklaying, Masonry, Slating, Plastering, Painting, Smithing, and Turning. Containing a full Description of the Tools belonging to each Branch of Business, and copious Directions for their Use: with an Explanation of the Terms used in each Art; and an Introduction to Practical Geometry. Illustrated by 39 Plates. By *Peter Nicholson*. Octavo, 18s. Boards, 21s. Bound.

An Essay on the Shafts of Mills; containing their Description and Use, with the Kinds of Stress to which they are subject, and an Inquiry into their Stiffness, Strength, Durability, and Proportion. With a Variety of useful Tables. Also an introductory Account of the Progress and Improvement of MILL-WORK. By *Robertson Buchanan*, Engineer. Illustrated with Three Plates, Price 7s. Boards.

Essays on the Construction and Durability of the Longitudinal Connexions of Shafts denominated Couplings.—On Methods of Disengaging and Re-engaging Machinery, while in Motion.—On Mechanism for Equalizing the Motion of Mills, denominated Lift-Tenters, Engine Governors, and Water-Wheel Governors.—On the Velocity of Water-Wheels.—On Changing the Velocity of Machinery while in Motion.—On the Framing of Mill-Work.
By

By *Robertson Buchanan*, Engineer. Illustrated with 15 Plates, Price 12s. in Boards.

Curr's Coal Viewer and Engine Builder's Practical Companion. Quarto, 2l. 12s. 6d.

Smeaton's Experiments on Under-shot and Over-shot Water Wheels, &c. Octavo, with five Plates, 10s. 6d. Boards.

Experimental Enquiries concerning the Principle of the lateral Communication of Motion in Fluids; applied to the Explanation of various Hydraulic Phenomena. By *J. P. Venturi*. Translated from the French by *W. Nicholson*, with Plates, 4s.

A Treatise on the *Teeth of Wheels*, *Pinions*, &c. demonstrating the best Form which can be given them for the various Purposes of Machinery; such as Mill-work, Clock-work, &c. and the Art of finding their Numbers, translated from the French of *M. Camus*, with Additions, illustrated by 15 Plates, Octavo, 10s. 6d.

Observations on the *Design for the Theatre Royal, Drury Lane*, as executed in the Year 1812; accompanied by Plans, Elevations, and Sections of the same, engraved on Eighteen Plates. By *Benjamin Wyatt*, F. S. A. Architect. Royal Quarto, 2l. 12s. 6d. Boards.

The Arabian Antiquities of Spain, representing, on 100 Engravings, the principal Remains of Architecture, Sculpture, Paintings, and Mosaics, of the Spanish Arabs, from Drawings made on the spot. By *James Cavanah Murphy*, Architect. Large Folio, half-bound.

JUST PUBLISHED.

THE ELGIN MARBLES of the Temple of Minerva at Athens, engraved on Sixty-One Plates, selected from Stuart and Revett's Antiquities of Athens; to which are added, the Report from the Select Committee of the House of Commons respecting the Earl of Elgin's Collection of Sculptured Marbles, and an Historical Account of the Temple. Imperial Quarto, Price 5l. 5s. Boards.

Fragments on the *Theory and Practice of Landscape Gardening*, including some Remarks on Grecian and Gothic Architecture, collected from various Manuscripts in the possession of the different Noblemen and Gentlemen for whose Use they were originally written; the Whole tending to establish fixed principles in the respective Arts. By *H. Repton*, Esq., assisted by his Son, *J. Adey Repton*, F. A. S. In Imperial Quarto, illustrated with Fifty-Two Plates, many of them elegantly coloured, uniformly with his former Works, Price 6l. 6s. Boards.

Remarks on the *Construction of Hot-Houses*, pointing out the most advantageous Forms, Materials, and Contrivances, to be used in their Construction. Also, a Review of the various Methods of building them in foreign Countries, as well as in England. With 10 Plates, from Etchings on Stone. By *I. C. Loudon*, F. L. S. Quarto, 15s. Boards.

An Essay on the *Strength and Stress of Timber*, founded upon Experiments performed at the Royal Military Academy, on Specimens selected from the Royal Arsenal, and his Majesty's Dock Yard at Woolwich; preceded by an Historical Review of former Theories and Experiments. Also, an Appendix on the Strength of Iron, and other Materials. By *Peter Barlow*, of the Royal Military Academy. Octavo, with numerous Tables and Plates, Price 18s. in Boards.

Plans, Elevations, and Sections of Buildings, Public and Private, executed in various parts of England, &c. including the *New Custom House, London*, with Plans, Details, and Descriptions. By *David Laing*, F. S. A. Architect and Surveyor to the Board of Customs. Elegantly engraved on 59 Plates. Imperial Folio, Price 5l. 5s. in Boards.

Designs for Churches and Chapels, including Plans, Elevations, and Sections, with some Sketches for Altars and Pulpits. By *W. F. Pocock*, Architect. Engraved on 44 Quarto Plates. Price 1l. 11s. 6d. in Boards.

A View of *the Cast Iron Bridge erected over the River Thames at Vauxhall*, elegantly engraved in Aquatinta, from a Drawing by *E. Gyfford*, Architect. Price 1l. 1s. or coloured impressions, 1l. 11s. 6d.

PREPARING FOR PUBLICATION.

Elementary Principles of Carpentry, &c. with Plates, by *T. Tredgold*. Quarto.

FINIS.